MW00532485

Positioning for Advantage

POSITIONING FOR ADVANTAGE

Techniques and Strategies to Grow Brand Value

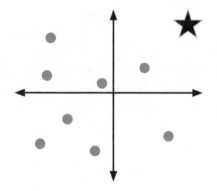

KIMBERLY A. WHITLER

Columbia University Press
Publishers Since 1893
New York   Chichester, West Sussex
cup.columbia.edu

Copyright © 2021 Columbia University Press
All rights reserved

Library of Congress Cataloging-in-Publication Data
Names: Whitler, Kimberly A., author.
Title: Positioning for advantage : techniques and strategies to
grow brand value / Kimberly A. Whitler.
Description: New York : Columbia University Press, [2021] |
Includes bibliographical references and index.
Identifiers: LCCN 2020056646 (print) | LCCN 2020056647 (ebook) |
ISBN 9780231189002 (hardback ; alk. paper) | ISBN 9780231548113 (ebook)
Subjects: LCSH: Brand name products—Management. | Branding (Marketing) |
Product management.
Classification: LCC HD69.B7 W45 2021 (print) | LCC HD69.B7 (ebook) |
DDC 658.8/27—dc23
LC record available at https://lccn.loc.gov/2020056646
LC ebook record available at https://lccn.loc.gov/2020056647

Columbia University Press books are printed on permanent
and durable acid-free paper.
Printed in the United States of America

Cover design: Noah Arlow

Contents

Contents

Acknowledgments

I have been beyond fortunate to have had countless colleagues and advisers who influenced my professional and intellectual growth throughout my life. Although it is impossible to acknowledge the hundreds of executives who have been interviewed, the number of faculty and professional colleagues who have fostered my growth, and the innumerable students with whom I have had the pleasure to work, I want to recognize a few consequential individuals who have helped bring this book to life.

First, thanks go to members of the University of Virginia Darden Business School community who have been deeply involved, including a number of students who have conducted research, provided input, and read excerpts to ensure clarity: Ellen Regan, Stephen Mann, Adrian Viesca Trevino, Kirstin DeCecca, Mark Pohl, Kate Maxwell, Kyle Wyper, and Wilkerson Anthony. Sarah Young, an undergraduate research assistant at UVA, has been especially helpful conducting research, reviewing and checking figures, references, and images. I have worked with Sarah for nearly two years and she is an extraordinary talent.

Second, I thank the friends, colleagues, CMOs, and CEOs who have provided insight along the way. Although too numerous to cite, there are certain individuals who repeatedly shared their unique insight: Scott Brinker, Marsha Collier, Steven Cook, Christine DeYoung, Caren Fleit, Brian Hansberry, Bob Huth, Antonio Lucio, Tamara McCleary, Gene Morphis, Drew Neisser, Scott Vaughan, Greg Welch, Dan White, and FD Wilder.

Third, I thank the individuals who were formative early in my career—whose lessons still matter: Jeff Vicek (the absolute best economics professor), Rick Thompson (the perfect summer intern and first boss), and Deb Henretta (the best early-career mentor one could want). I was fortunate to start at Procter and Gamble and to learn what strategic growth engineering was all about from dozens of excellent leaders.

Fourth, I want to express special gratitude to the number of scholars who have inspired me throughout my second career as a professor: Ken Bernhardt, Robin Coulter, John Deighton, Peter Golder, Mark Houston, Bernie Jaworski, Kevin Keller, Kay Lemon, Leigh McAlister, Chris Moorman, Linda Price, and Rebecca Slotegraaf. And gratitude also to my co-authors, from whom I have learned much: Ali Besharat, Paul Farris, Hui Feng, Saim Kashmiri, Ryan Krause, Don Lehmann, Neil Morgan, Lopo Rego, and Matt Semadeni. Of special note is Bob Lusch, a giant of a scholar and an even better man. It was his encouragement to pursue a PhD and his guidance throughout the process that enabled me to fulfill a lifelong dream.

Finally, endless gratitude goes to Chris Puto—my lifelong mentor and friend who is the most patient and kind person you will ever meet (and absolutely the best editor around)—and to my parents, Carol Ann and Robert Whitler. I learned to *love* learning from my mother. To this day, my mother always has a book in her hands or is playing some sort of game. Her passion for knowledge and intellectual growth has always been inspirational and contagious. From my father, I learned that success is earned the hard way. His focus on setting goals and measuring performance, the dedication and hours that he put in, and his kindness to all people throughout the journey served as a tremendous model. And to my sister, Janis, who has endured more of life's challenges than anybody should. She has taught me to fight, to never give up, and to never stop smiling—no matter what.

I am deeply indebted to the people who have not only provided input on this project but also have inspired and supported me along the way.

Positioning for Advantage

INTRODUCTION AND
ORGANIZING FRAMEWORK

1

The Marketing Impact Framework

Over the years, I have watched closely the types of marketers who have successfully ascended into CEO roles. Of course, the inherent DNA of the leader (him or herself) plays the central role in this but it is also clear that certain companies and/or sectors also improve one's chances as well. Of note would be a handful of top CPG companies like P&G, PepsiCo and Kraft Heinz who historically have done an excellent job of developing well rounded leaders. Importantly, these complex and sophisticated environments, where marketing leaders truly play the lead role in the P&L management, would appear to be an excellent training ground.

—GREG WELCH, PARTNER AT SPENCER STUART, ONE OF THE
WORLD'S LARGEST EXECUTIVE SEARCH FIRMS[1]

WHY DOES TIDE HAVE a superior brand image as compared to Wisk? How did marketers create a Nike brand that dominates many of the categories in which it competes? How have Apple and Microsoft effectively staked out unique market positions, enabling both to thrive? And how have both Amazon and Walmart developed brands that have greater revenue, market value, and market share than Target or Kmart?

For many observers, successful brand building seems like luck. But for well-trained marketing strategists, it is the result of using a series of consumer-based, science-backed tools to help create a blueprint of the desired brand and then leveraging all of a firm's resources to construct the brand in a unified manner. As John Deighton, professor emeritus at Harvard Business School, suggests, "Strong brands are a reward."[2] Such a brand is the result of defining a superior position, constructing a strong brand essence statement (BES), and then working uniformly—across all functions—to implement the desired brand.

Yet, superior brand building remains a mystery. A common question that I hear from students and managers alike is, "What is it that marketers do?" And I tell them that they seek to create businesses—through brands—that win in the marketplace. While firm leaders are aware that marketers are responsible for brand development, what remains elusive is how to do so in a way that creates a sustainable competitive advantage.

In a review that I made of more than 500 chief marketing officer (CMO) profiles on LinkedIn, less than 10 percent had a degree in marketing. This means that most people who lead the marketing function in companies don't have a degree in marketing—imagine if most chief finance officers (CFOs) didn't have a finance degree! And those who did study marketing in college or graduate school rarely, if ever, had courses that focused on how to *do* marketing. Most undergraduate courses tend to be theory or concept based, with few using tools and workshops to teach students how to create, build, or construct successful brands. Consequently, the vast majority of marketers discover what marketing is, and how to create marketing strategies and plans, from their employers on the job.

This can be problematic, as firms vary in their marketing capability. The consequence, therefore, is that the quality of training that new marketing employees receive can vary significantly. Some firms are known for having a superior marketing capability—and therefore offering better training—but most firms are not. In research that I conducted with Christine DeYoung, partner at DHR International, a global executive recruiting firm, to identify the top-ranked companies for developing C-level marketing leaders, almost all of them were from the consumer package goods (CPG) or retailing industry.[3] More recently, I analyzed LinkedIn data to identify the firms that do the best job of preparing marketers to become chief executive officers (CEOs) (see figure 1.1). As you look at the top fifteen, notice who *isn't* on the list. Where are the leading technology, consulting, or business-to-business (B2B) firms? Of course, this may change over time as some of the younger technology firms develop structured, disciplined,

4

FIGURE 1.1 Companies that best prepare marketers to become CEOs

and sophisticated marketing methods that create employees who can reach the C-suite. But today, they aren't generally considered to have the best-in-class training that helps prepare marketers to lead a firm.

What do these developers of C-level marketing talent have in common? They all have systematic and science-based systems, processes, and approaches to building superior brands. Almost all have decades of experience, libraries of best practices, and expert marketers who can help train and develop young talent. The marketers in these firms are typically profit and loss (P&L) leaders in their firms and play an upstream role, often being expected to lead the development of the strategic plans that will drive growth. This differs from the nearly

50 percent of companies that treat marketing as only a sales activity, existing just to commercialize the products that other firm leaders create.[4] In such scenarios, marketers are typically isolated in downstream roles, with others in the firms defining the strategic direction and developing the innovation pipeline.

Deb Henretta, former group president at Procter & Gamble (P&G), says, "Procter and Gamble's Brand Management organization has proven to be a great training ground for marketing executives and C-suite executives alike. Deeply rooted in the consumer, P&G marketers learn how to glean powerful business insights and use them to create leading-edge product and marketing innovations that drive sustainable top-line and bottom-line results. These experiences produce powerful business and marketing leaders capable of building iconic brands."[5]

Eduardo Luz, former U.S. CMO at Kraft Heinz, provides this perspective:

Under our value of Ownership, we keep brand decisions as close as possible to local markets and consumers. To make sure we're constantly elevating our game across 200 brands in 125 countries, we provide our Marketing teams with tools, content, and decision frameworks that reflect the "KHC Way of Marketing", a proprietary approach that we're now rolling out globally (after piloting in the US). Under our value of Meritocracy, we reward Marketers who drive industry-leading results with accelerated responsibilities and promotions. Because our Marketers are equipped and incentivized to think and act like owners of their brands and businesses, they're well-prepared to move into the ranks of senior management and the C-suite.[6]

Christine DeYoung states:

Few businesses allow a new manager in the company to train to be a GM—full accountability across a whole team. Most companies are set up very functionally until the SVP level—which then often needs to be brought in from the outside as they only have functional experts. To be a CEO, you need to be able to develop strategies that generate profitable growth, motivate, and inspire an entire organization to want to deliver, and understand how the pieces and parts of the organization fit together to achieve excellent execution. The best firms put marketers in what I call mini-CEO positions, often called brand management positions within the CPG industry. There aren't many firms that put marketers in these roles, but those that do enable their alumni to go on to ascend to CEO roles. One factor that is critical to remember is that most of the very top firms have long legacies—they have decades of alumni who have ascended to CEO positions. As recruiters, this provides data and insight into the firms that better prepare young marketers to become successful CEOs.[7]

What all this suggests is that there are a few firms that have a track record of developing marketing talent who can develop the strategies and plans to drive growth and lead the rest of the organization to execute effectively. These successful firms are distinguished by the methods they use to do marketing, refined over decades of testing, and are not available in textbooks or general business books.

In contrast, the marketing curriculum in schools is largely theory based, with little insight into the tools that marketers can employ to create brand advantage. For example, consider Michael Porter's strategy typology or the BCG matrix (developed by the Boston Consulting Group). Many students learn about Porter's strategies (i.e., low cost strategy, focus strategy, and differentiated strategy) for pursuing competitive advantage. The BCG matrix, which introduces students to the concepts of "stars," "cash cows," "question marks," and "dogs," is another useful framework to begin understanding how brands can play different roles within a portfolio. These theoretical frameworks are important foundational concepts to help students understand the strategic choices they can make. However, once the frameworks are understood, students should learn how to create a differentiated brand positioning—or how to create a strategic positioning that gives a brand the chance to become a star. Unfortunately, there aren't many tools or guides that help students or practicing marketers understand how to do this. I call this the "theory-doing gap," or the inability to convert general marketing concepts into successful business practices.

To put this into perspective, I graduated with a double major in psychology and business administration. I had a lot of training in statistics and human behavior, which I connected with my degree in business administration. I then got a master's of business administration (MBA) and took as many finance and marketing courses as possible, pursuing both career paths. After I got job offers in both finance and general management marketing, a professor I respected, Dr. Chris Puto, advised me to take the brand management offer from P&G because "they would provide the best general management marketing training." As he explained, MBA programs provide students with conceptual, strategic, and analytical thinking skills while honing their ability to work effectively with others. They can't teach students how to be a marketer at a start-up, Google, P&G, or Amazon because marketing at these firms varies.

Dr. Puto was right. While I had a lot of academic training in psychology and business administration, I was unprepared to actually do marketing. P&G took a rigorous, systematic, replicable, and analytical approach to building brands. They incorporated art and science in a methodical way in order to understand consumers, the marketplace, and competitors. They had a uniform method for teaching brand management employees how to create growing businesses. Part of this was through daily interaction, questioning, and coaching from the manager.

Part of P&G's method included classes that all brand management employees took at different points in their development. Much of that training was through the consistent use of key tools and documents across all brands, business units, and geographies. Whether you worked on Tide in the United States or Biomat in the Czech Republic, the format for defining a brand was the same and the data required to prove that your brand had a superior positioning strategy did not vary. The process—gathering consumer insights, converting them into a superior position, and then defining the brand blueprint—was consistent. More often than not, the uniform process, training, and tools led to market share leadership. P&G, which has thrived for over 180 years, has a portfolio of twenty-three billion-dollar brands and another fourteen with sales of $500 million to $1 billion.[8]

This book is designed to fill the theory-doing gap by providing a series of analytical, conceptual, and executional methods (which, for clarity, I will call "tools") designed to help aspiring C-level marketers. It is the culmination of over 400 interviews with C-level leaders, consulting engagements with companies across different industries, and my former experience as a general manager / CMO and current experience as a professor. I will provide insights into how to use a number of methods and tools to build a superior brand that achieves positional advantage.

How Marketers Uniquely Contribute to Firm Advantage

To understand the tools that marketers use to create advantage, it's important to understand *what* marketers uniquely contribute to firm performance. In other words, if you removed marketers from firms, what would change? Figure 1.2 helps explain how well-trained and proficient marketers create a sustainable competitive advantage for firms at which they work.[9] Specifically, marketers create advantage by combining the firm's resources with insight-generating market intelligence (e.g., competitors and consumers) and direction from firm-level strategies in order to make strategic marketing choices about where the brand should play, or its desired positioning. Better marketers are able to generate superior market-based insights that enable them to identify a desired positioning that will lead to brand advantage.

The goal is to make strategic decisions regarding the desired consumer target, positioning territory, and brand essence that are unique,

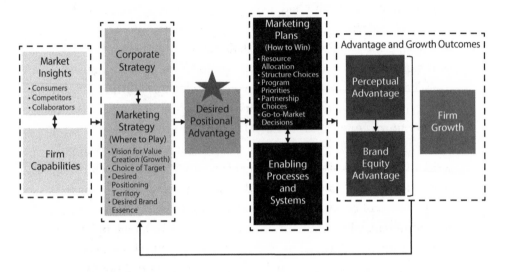

FIGURE 1.2 The marketing impact framework
Source: Created by the author

ownable, and relevant. The result leads to a "desired positional advantage," or the potential to occupy a place in the hearts and minds of the target consumers that gives the company the ability to achieve superior market share outcomes. This is important. Identifying the desired positioning is the first step in achieving actual brand advantage. Marketing strategy is simply a paper-based blueprint of where you want the brand to play. It defines the cognitive space that the brand hopes to achieve among consumers. But it must be activated or implemented effectively to do so.

Activation requires the development and implementation of smart marketing plans that can achieve the desired positioning. Marketing plans, then, set the boundary for the "how to win" choices and include decisions regarding resource allocation (both human and financial), program priorities (e.g., promotional, pricing, and product decisions), organizational structure design (i.e., what is outsourced, which functions report to marketing, and so forth), strategic partners (e.g., Coca-Cola's partnership with *American Idol*), and go-to-market activities (e.g., how to distribute, or get the product or service to the consumer).

In the aggregate, these choices are what the marketing team implements to achieve the desired positional advantage and can be helped (or hindered) by the enabling processes and systems. As an example of a process that can affect implementation, I worked on a brand at one point where the advertising development process was slow, frustrating (for both the creatives and the client), and expensive. Moreover, the process was failing to deliver the desired advertising results, preventing the brand team from achieving the desired positioning. Because the process was getting in the way of results, we designed a project to improve the advertising development process. These enabling structures can make a significant difference in whether the marketer's strategy and plans can achieve advantage.

The outcome of superior marketing strategies and plans is perceptual advantage (in the hearts and minds of consumers), which translates into brand equity advantage and ultimately drives growth. Whether somebody is playing chess, fighting on the battlefield, or attempting to create preference among target consumers, the objective is the same—to create a vision of how they will win given their competitive set and then effectively activate the vision to achieve victory.

How the Book Is Organized

This book is designed to provide specific tools that marketers can use to create positional advantage, brand advantage, and firm growth. Consequently, there are three types of tools—marketing strategy tools, bridging tools, and planning tools—that align with the general marketing activities in the marketing impact framework (see figure 1.3).

Chapters 2–4 introduce tools focused on identifying and creating positional advantage—essentially tools designed to help determine marketing strategy. If you want to find a position that is unique and relevant to your target, the starting point is to identify the specific positioning

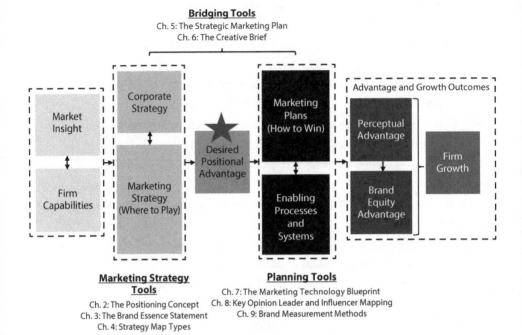

FIGURE 1.3 How the book chapters align with the marketing impact framework

and brand architecture. Or if you want to grow your business by being relevant to more consumers, the starting point is to identify how you will enlarge your positioning and shift your brand architecture so it is more compelling to a larger audience. Chapters 2–4 provide specific tools to help you specify your desired positioning (chapter 2), define your brand essence statement (chapter 3), and use strategy mapping to help communicate, align, and sell your strategic thinking (chapter 4).

Specifically, chapter 2 introduces a tool that enables you to create and test a strategic positioning concept for a brand, service, or experience. This discussion helps marketers understand that a marketing strategy requires establishing the central position for a brand relative to its competitors in a way that creates meaningful value for consumers. Once the position, or desired territory that you want to own (relative to competitors), is determined, the next step is to convert the positioning into the pieces and parts of a brand. If Coca-Cola wants to own "refreshment" in the hearts and minds of consumers, how do they build a brand that can do this? What benefit must the brand offer the consumer? What values and personality should it have?

Chapter 3 builds on these tools by explaining how to convert a desired position into a brand architecture. To help marketers become more proficient at communicating their desired positioning, chapter 4 provides a framework and examples for the different types of strategy maps that marketers can use to inform internal and external stake-holders. Identifying the desired position and constructing the brand essence are useful for marketers. However, to drive firm-level commitment, alignment, and adoption, marketers have to effectively "sell" their work. Chapter 4 arms marketers with tools that can be used to help drive enterprise-wide support.

While chapters 2–4 provide tools to help define, construct, and communicate the desired positional advantage, chapters 5 and 6 provide bridging tools to help marketers understand how to convert strategy into plans. Specifically, once Coca-Cola determines the brand essence that they want to own, the next step is to define plans that will ensure success. The importance of this cannot be overstated. Coca-Cola's desire to own "refreshment" is one thing, but actually doing so requires excellent implementation of the plans designed to achieve the strategies.

Chapter 5 provides a structure and approach for creating a strategic marketing plan—or the choices that a marketer makes about how to build a brand so that it achieves positional advantage. Chapter 6 builds on chapter 5 by describing the creative brief, which can help marketers ensure that their strategic choices are implemented effectively. If a strategic priority consists of implementing a new technology, developing a new marketing campaign, or creating a new influencer marketing program, the creative brief is the tool that defines the project parameters required to ensure success.

After you have gained insight into the tools that help bridge the marketing strategy and planning processes, chapters 7–9 go on to describe tools that can help aid in the development of contemporary marketing plans. While there are thousands of possible tactics that marketers could employ, the focus is on three that are very common across firms and industries. Specifically, chapter 7 defines the Marketing and Technology (MarTech) Blueprint, a tool that marketers are beginning to use to understand how marketing and technology interact to affect both the company and the consumer. Given the critical interconnectedness between marketing and technology, this tool is one that almost any marketer can use if their strategic priority is to identify and/or implement new technology.

Following the MarTech Blueprint, the Influencer Mapping tool is introduced in chapter 8. Historically important in B2B firms, influencer marketing has grown in popularity through the power of social media. Today, brands of all stripes, with many Asian companies leading the way, are integrating influencer marketing programs to achieve positional advantage. The Influencer Mapping tool helps provide specific guidance for aligning marketing actions.

Chapter 9 wraps up the marketing process by addressing the final priority that marketers across firms and industries are emphasizing: the need to be more accountable. Because the objective of marketing is to create positional advantage, marketers are challenged to demonstrate impact. I will provide a framework for and insight into a number of methods that marketers can use to measure brand health, positional advantage, and financial performance, which will provide a way to think about what metrics are available so you can choose the right ones for your circumstances.

The final chapter, chapter 10, provides advice and exercises on how to practice using the tools, helping you to achieve a degree of proficiency that will ensure better in-market results. There are recommended steps that marketers can take to practice reverse engineering a BES or identifying a competitor's positioning concept. There are tips to think about how to identify the optimal creative brief for your business circumstances. Because this book is about bridging the theory-doing gap, this last chapter is filled with ideas on how to build your competency.

As you read through the book, keep in mind that some of the tools define a specific method for accomplishing a marketing task. For example, in chapter 2, the strategic positioning concept tool is introduced, which is a specific method for creating, testing, and determining whether a positioning territory is effective. In other chapters, such as in chapters 4 and 9, a number of common examples of the tool are provided rather than a single, detailed exemplar. Whether there is a single tool or a series of examples primarily depends on whether the tool is flexible and can be used across different situations or if it is more context dependent.

In the aggregate, this book is designed to provide a foundational understanding of the key tools that marketers from more sophisticated companies, like those in figure 1.1, are likely to use. While it is based on sound theory, it bridges the theory-doing gap by introducing specific yet flexible tools that can help you implement marketing strategies and plans. Whether you are a seasoned marketer or a novice—or you just work with marketers—this book is designed to move beyond theory and help you better understand how to employ the right marketing tools to have more success creating, building, and growing brands.

MARKETING STRATEGY TOOLS

2

The Positioning Concept

Most companies focus on product development—how to create a superior product. However, great marketing companies know that a truly superior positioning concept, anchored in deep consumer insight, is what should lead a successful product development process. Unfortunately, most companies don't know how to create a superior positioning concept.

—LEE SUSEN, CHIEF SALES AND MARKETING
OFFICER FOR MCILHENNY[1]

IN SCHOOLS AROUND THE world, sophisticated classes are being developed to help budding entrepreneurs learn how to create new products. These classes focus on topics such as the product-development process, the importance of prototyping and testing products, and even newer methods for innovation such as agile development. However, while individuals are focused on developing new products, a gap remains regarding how to create, test, and perfect the core positioning of the brand—or the definition of where the brand should be "located" conceptually (i.e., stand for) in the hearts and minds of consumers relative to competitors. This positioning concept should set the boundary and guide the product that is actually created.

This gap in understanding may be one of the most important reasons that up to 90 percent of new products fail.[2] While it is obvious to most businesspeople that the design of a new product requires development, testing, and iteration, very few are taught to understand why it is as important to use a similarly rigorous process to define the strategic positioning that will guide all decisions—from the product to the brand design (i.e., the brand essence statement [BES]) to the choice of commercialization strategies and tactics.

So why aren't leaders leveraging the power of superior positioning to drive firm, government, and organizational advantage? Is it lack of skill? Lack of will? Lack of time? Or the fact that this topic isn't taught in higher education, leaving it for managers to figure it out? While these are contributing factors, the reality is that creating a superior positioning concept is significantly more difficult than most people think. "Superior," after all, means that a positioning concept for Tide must be better than the positioning statements written by the talented brand managers working on competitive brands such as All, Wisk, Cheer, and Era. To begin the journey of understanding how to create superior positioning, this chapter introduces the idea of a positioning concept, the elements of a positioning concept, and the attributes of concepts that tend to be superior to those of their rivals.

What Is a Positioning Concept, and Why Is It Important?

A "positioning concept" is a tool that enables leaders to create, test, and perfect the *ideas* upon which new brands and/or products are created and launched. It identifies the consumer's problem, the solution that your brand is designed to provide, and proof that the brand can deliver. It essentially summarizes why your brand exists—and places it conceptually relative to competitors—in a way that is anchored on the consumer's needs.

Many entrepreneurs make the mistake of anchoring on the development of a new product, failing to connect the value of the benefit that the product creates to the *market* for the solution. When leaders focus on developing a product, it's possible that there won't be a real consumer need. In other words, when the product is created, the market demand is negligible—which could have been identified at the beginning had the leaders identified and then tested the positioning concept. They would have figured out that a market didn't exist before they invested any money in developing an unneeded product.

To make this point more vivid, consider the following two stories. During the winter of 2010, an Indiana University senior, Derek Pacque, was enjoying a night out with his friends. He left his coat in the corner of a nightclub, and when he went to find it at the end of the evening, his coat was gone. A new product idea was born out of the entrepreneur's personal experience, and he launched Hoosier Coat Check. After struggling to find a lucrative and sizable market, Derek renamed the firm CoatChex and sought to change and expand the product offering.[3] This is common among entrepreneurs; through personal experience, they identify an opportunity for a new product and begin developing it.

Consider an alternative approach. A large, global firm is deciding which of hundreds of new product ideas to focus its research and development efforts on. It conducts a global needs–delivery gap assessment, determining what problems (i.e., needs) are most important to consumers and which of these problems aren't being solved by current products. Based on this insight, marketers then "size the market" for each opportunity—they generate rough estimates of the potential revenue that each idea could generate. Included in this assessment is an understanding of the competitors' strategic positioning, product-innovation pipelines, and core competencies. After a thorough analysis, marketers rank the broad product opportunities based on a number of criteria (e.g., fit with firm competency and market potential) to determine the new product opportunity (i.e., white space) on which the company will focus its resources. At this point, the company does two things: it develops many positioning concepts that define the central idea behind the product, and then, after prioritizing the best concepts, it commissions engineers to prototype the product.

The first story represents a process anchored on an entrepreneur's experience, while the second hinges on a data-based assessment of the consumers, competitors, and market for a prospective product. While both can be successful (consider Facebook as a good example of the former approach), the latter approach, more disciplined and market-centered, is less risky because it is based on more than one individual's life experience and applies a lot of market-based data to determine where to invest resources. The second approach also increases the likelihood that the entrepreneur will become more than a one-hit wonder.

As mentioned in chapter 1, the industry with the best reputation for employing superior marketing techniques to achieve business results, and consequently doing the best job at developing marketers, has historically been the consumer package goods (CPG) industry.[4] Although many industries and companies do not employ concept development in their product-ideation process, the world's most renowned firms, such as Coca-Cola, Unilever, General Mills, E&J Gallo, Procter & Gamble (P&G), and Johnson & Johnson, have been using the concept development process to lead the design and development of new product introductions for decades. While it is well known that leading firms use science to create the next breakthrough product, it is less clear how they use science to develop an idea that identifies the position against which the product should be designed.

Why does a superior positioning concept matter? The science behind generating a superior concept is rigorous,[5] can be time consuming, and is far more challenging than nonmarketers understand. As mentioned earlier, up to 90 percent of all new products fail (the statistic varies based on the industry),[6] and less than 3 percent of new CPG products exceed first-year sales of $50 million,[7] demonstrating how difficult it is to achieve success. Many fail because the idea upon which the product is launched is not compelling, relevant, or important to consumers; because the size of the potential market for the idea is small; because the product doesn't effectively deliver the positioning concept; or because of poor implementation (e.g., weak marketing communication). Is it worth putting all that time and energy into a concept that has a very small chance of succeeding in the first place?

In the Hoosier Coat Check scenario mentioned previously, the product was featured on ABC's Shark Tank and investor Mark Cuban valued the innovation at \$600,000.[8] The product ultimately failed to achieve widespread success, most likely because the central idea—not the developed application, which Cuban praised—wasn't important to consumers or the restaurants and other venues that would have to implement it. A rigorous concept development process could have helped determine the degree and size of appeal (i.e., market size potential) before time and money were invested in product development. While the founder has changed the firm name and continued to evolve and expand the product to try and find a sizable market, a positioning concept could have ultimately saved him time (or helped him understand that it wasn't worth investing in).

Who Is Responsible for Developing a Positioning Concept?

While the person responsible for developing a positioning concept can vary by firm, the marketing function typically owns the development, ideation, testing, and refinement of the concept. In fact, a primary function that marketing departments manage across companies is the positioning of a brand and its related products and services. Representatives from a marketing department then work with the engineers who are building the product to ensure that it delivers on the final positioning concept chosen.

The Process of Positioning Concept Development

As previously mentioned, many firms do not have a process for developing positioning concepts, but those that have developed a standardized approach differ in their methods, in part because the process is not typically taught in higher education or via books. As a result, there is tremendous variance in competency and outcomes across positioning concepts. However, most sophisticated firms will go through a process to identify (1) the consumer problem (in clear, articulated, and

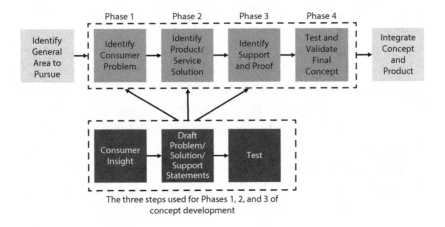

The three steps used for Phases 1, 2, and 3 of
concept development

FIGURE 2.1 The process of developing the positioning concept
Source: Created by the author

written statements); (2) the solution; and (3) the proof that the solution addresses the consumer problem (see figure 2.1). It is an iterative process that requires deep consumer insight, and when done correctly, can be consumer-tested throughout to assess the brand's appeal and potential.

Before the process starts, it is critical to prioritize the criteria against which the new concept will be judged. This requires generating broad insight and alignment from key stakeholders, and then identifying which of the opportunities meets success criteria and should therefore be taken to the concept development phase. This prioritization step is one that many smaller and entrepreneurial firms ignore. Instead, they tend to lock in on an exciting opportunity, but then they fail to compare the idea to others generated—against established criteria—to ensure that the product they develop has the best chance for achieving success. I once heard an executive tell his organization, "Big dogs have big puppies." His point was that holding everything else constant, the best technology and the biggest opportunities should be the priorities. This came on the heels of a strategic mistake—one in which a category had paired a high-opportunity technology with a smaller brand (rather than putting the technology on the brand that had the leading market share). While not the focus of this chapter, becoming adept at rationally and objectively evaluating market opportunities is a skill that the most successful firms have developed. It must be based on an understanding of the external marketplace and the target consumer and requires marketers to stay anchored on the data—and detached from their own personal opinions.

Once the priorities are decided upon and the white-space opportunity (i.e., a new-to-the-world opportunity) is identified (referred to as the "general area to pursue" in this model), the concept development process can begin with the following four key phases.

Phase 1: Identify the Consumer Problem

The first phase of concept development is designed to identify the consumer problem that the new product, service, or experience is supposed to solve. For example, a potential problem statement in the laundry detergent category could be: "After I wash my clothes, they become stiff and brittle, uncomfortable to wear. I wish there was a laundry detergent that made my clothes more 'wearable'—soft and supple." This anchors on the consumer rather than the product and helps distinguish the marketing firms that focus on understanding the consumer problem (an outside-in approach) rather than the function of the product (an inside-out approach). To identify the consumer problem, a marketer gathers consumer insight, works with a team to draft problem statements, and tests the dozens of developed ideas to identify which are most important, unmet by competition, and differentiating. Once this is done, the marketer settles on a couple of problem statements with the highest potential to take to the next phase: generating solution statements.

To collect insight from consumers, marketers will look to multiple sources, such as listening to consumers (via focus groups or one-on-one interviews), observing consumers (via ethnographies), and analyzing consumer data (i.e., social media data, chat room data, scanner data, survey data, third-party data, first-party data, and purchase behavior data). While marketers lead this process, they should have a cross-functional team that participates in analyzing consumers and creating testable statements.

The goal of this research is to extract deep insight; by including scientists, creatives, technologists, operators, and even finance experts, marketers will be better able to generate a more holistic understanding of the consumer problem or need. Further, superior concept-generating ability can come from unexpected places. Throughout my professional career, I have developed hundreds of positioning concept statements and worked with a number of individuals across various functions. I tended to find talent in the most unexpected areas. At one point, I found that my counterpart in finance, the chief financial officer (CFO), had a particularly good understanding of marketing, so I sought out his insight regularly. At another point, a product-development engineer was an excellent wordsmith and idea generator. Part of the marketer's job is to find concept development talent wherever it may exist and employ these people to generate the best ideas.

After generating insight, the concept development team begins writing dozens of problem statements (i.e., a statement regarding the consumer problem that the product will solve), getting qualitative consumer feedback on everything from the overall message to word choice, as changing just one word in a problem statement could significantly alter the degree to which consumers agree. Once the final problem statements are developed, the team then tests them to identify which best connect with the target.

There are a number of methods to test these problem statement, and any company can employ a simple survey-based design that asks consumers to respond to a series of questions such as the following: How important is this problem to you? If a brand/product could solve this problem, how likely would you be to purchase it?

In general, a survey should capture both attitudinal measures toward the idea (e.g., likability and believability) and behavioral intent measures (e.g., purchase intent or intent to visit a retailer).

Phase 2: Develop Solution Statements

Phase 1 is completed as marketers analyze the testing data and determine the problem statements that are most relevant and motivating for consumers. This sets up the consumer-framed problem that the balance of the concept (and ultimately the product) must solve. Phase 2 of the concept development process involves identifying the solution statements that address the consumer-framed problem, as articulated in phase 1. Following the same process as described previously (i.e., gathering insight from consumers, writing dozens of solution statements, and then quantitatively testing them), the objective is to arrive at the top-ranking solution statements. To continue with the previous example, one possible solution to the consumer problem would be something like this: "Introducing New Tide Clothing Relaxer, a liquid that you put in the washing machine to help make clothes more wearable."

Phase 3: Develop Support Statements

Once phase 2 is complete and the marketers have determined the best solution statement to the consumer-framed problem, phase 3 requires identifying the support—or proof—that will convince the target consumers that the product, service, or experience that has been created can solve the problem. For example, assume that a primary issue facing retired people is the task of finding the assisted living facility best suited to their needs. Assume that after rigorous consumer insight work is completed, the solution statement to this problem is, "Finally, there is a service that helps retirees identify and choose the best assisted living facility for them." It is one thing to suggest that this service is the "best," but why should retirees believe it? What proof can the company offer to convince consumers that it will keep the promise being made (i.e., the solution statement)? Now consider the Tide example. What type of proof would be sufficient to believe that clothes are more "wearable"? Is it an ingredient? Or an expert endorsement (e.g., Martha Stewart)? Or a side-by-side visual? Or product testing? There is an endless number of supporting statements, but which combination is: (1) most compelling to the target, and (2) potentially achievable? Following the same process as phases 1 and 2, the objective is to arrive at the top-ranked support statements.

Phase 4: Testing and Validation of the Developed Concepts

By this point, marketers should have developed and identified the biggest problem, solution, and support statements based on quantitative testing. The next step is to assemble the pieces into whole concepts. There may be anywhere from five to dozens of complete concepts which must be tested and validated to determine the optimal idea to commercialize. Testing and validation should include quantitative data that provides the following insight: (1) which of the complete concepts is strongest (e.g., most compelling and motivating) from a consumer perspective, (2) which beats the key competitors' concepts, and (3) which is most supportable in terms of what the product could actually deliver. In some cases, marketers will be required to demonstrate that any new positioning concept beats the last new product introduction—essentially, there may be an additional internal bar to clear at leading marketing companies on top of the consumer, competitor, and product thresholds.

This stage is critical, although few firms take the time to conduct positioning concept testing, let alone validation testing. If a company doesn't know how well an idea stacks up against an existing idea, a competitor's idea, or a consumer's needs, how can they possibly know if they should invest all their marketing and product development resources into the idea? This idea is the blueprint against which all activities are designed and communicated. If the core concept strategy is weak, then the supplemental investment in things like product development, advertising, social media, digital, website development, in-store activity, sales materials, and sales calls with channel members will be weak at best.

As an example, I accepted a chief marketing officer (CMO) position at a company in an industry in which I had no experience; I had little prior understanding of the company's consumers, competitors, or market. One of the first things I did was to look at the core positioning of the firm, as expressed through its communications. Having conducted hundreds of concept tests up to that point, I was able to reverse engineer the positioning of my firm relative to their key competitors. Once I did this, it was fairly apparent that their core positioning was inferior to many of their competitors. How could I tell? Because the solution statement was based on a problem that I hypothesized was much less important to the target consumers than the solution statements provided by our competitors. Once I spent time getting actual consumer data to test my hypothesis, I found that the solution wasn't important to the target consumers. What did matter, however, was the hundred-million-dollar-plus investment that the company was wasting every year communicating a positioning that wasn't compelling.

Another challenge facing marketers is the need to demonstrate the results, impact, and return on investment (ROI) of a particular investment. If marketers don't prove, through quantitative testing, that the strategic idea behind their marketing is superior, then the chief executive officer (CEO) and other C-level leaders are left to decide for themselves whether they believe that the marketing team developed a strong positioning direction. This puts marketers (and the positioning concept) at risk because the C-suite views the ideas generated through their own lens and perspective—not that of consumers. And in some cases, there may be passive resistance, as many in the C-suite don't actively support the efforts. Empirical proof of the direction's soundness can help drive support and advocacy within the organization.

Part of the problem is that many firms without competency in marketing will outsource concept development to another entity such as an advertising agency. Ad agencies may be creative, but strategic positioning and confirmatory testing are very different skills than developing a creative advertising campaign. Few external agencies know how to quantitatively test their ideas, and few will voluntarily do so without pressure from the client. What this means is that you will not know if their recommendation is compelling or better than that of their competitors. You won't even know if it is better than the current positioning.

And the consequence could be that it has in fact put the brand in a worse position. On top of that, it will likely lead to in-market inconsistency as the entire organization shifts to deliver on a new positioning, only to abandon it and shift again when the team realizes that the new direction isn't having a positive impact on company results. And it will likely lead to internal conflict, as many nonmarketers don't buy into the evolved positioning. Generating data that validates a proposed positioning concept direction is fundamentally required both to increase the likelihood of in-market success and to drive organizational alignment and commitment.

Ensure Concept-Product Fit and Commercialize the New Concept

The final, tested concept then becomes the basis for product development. Once the product is developed, marketers should test the positioning concept idea with the product to ensure optimal concept-product fit in the market, which will validate that the product delivers on the promise established in the positioning concepts. To test the fit, marketers typically work with the research and development (R&D) team to test the concept and the product together. Once the final concept-product match has been validated, the next step is to commercialize the new product by converting the concept into marketing communications (i.e., advertisements, social media, and public relations). Finally, the new brand or product is launched.

Developing the Problem, Solution, and Supporting Statements: An Example

The Problem Statement

The first stage of concept development is to develop several positioning concepts by effectively framing the problem using consumer language and insight. This is the anchor of the concept; it forces marketers to stay centered on solving consumer problems instead of their own. Specifically, the marketer needs to pinpoint the best way to articulate the problem so that it resonates with the greatest number of target consumers.

The problem statement should always be in the consumers' words, should simply state the core problem (as it relates to the product being introduced), and should frame the context for what comes next. How this idea is written affects whether it resonates with only a few target consumers or many—essentially determining the size of the market to which the idea will appeal.

Using a hypothetical example, assume that the brand manager of Smartwater (a bottled water produced and sold by Coca-Cola) wants to introduce a new line extension. Before a concept can be developed, it's imperative to prioritize the various new product areas on which to focus. Assume that in this example, the brand manager has consumer, competitor, and market data that identifies fifty new product ideas—everything from enhanced (e.g., electrolyte-infused) water and flavored water to new channel opportunities (e.g., new sizes for the club channel) and new packaging options. The brand manager's first job is to identify which of the myriad opportunities she should focus her organization's resources on—that is, which opportunity would appeal to the greatest number of consumers because it is solving the biggest "unmet" need. Then assume that after assessing the market potential of all fifty product ideas, the brand manager decides that the biggest new product opportunity is a self-chilling bottle.

The consumer problem associated with this opportunity is that the current Smartwater bottle (or any other plastic bottle, for that matter) doesn't stay cold after being removed from the refrigerator. In order to write a successful problem statement, the marketer would need to understand the full scope of the problem, how consumers use Smartwater (i.e., occasions, habits, and practices), what compensating behaviors they do in response to the problem (e.g., pouring Smartwater out of the bottle and into a glass with ice), how competitors have solved the problem (if indeed they have), and how the problem connects to other aspects of the consumer's life.

For example, consider the following four problem statements:

1. I don't like drinking water from packaged plastic bottles. I wish that there were a better type of packaging that made my water taste better.
2. I tend to sip my water throughout the day. Unfortunately, the water in my bottle gets warm quickly. I wish that there were a way to keep my water cold throughout the day.
3. I love cold water. Unfortunately, during the summer, it seems as if the water in my bottle gets warm as soon as I take it out of the refrigerator. I wish that there were a way to keep my water colder in the summer.
4. There is nothing better than ice-cold water right out of the refrigerator. It is the best-tasting water—crisp, fresh, and pure. Unfortunately, my water bottle starts warming up as soon as I take it out of the refrigerator. I wish that there were a way to keep my water colder so that it tasted better longer.

In evaluating these four problem statements, you can see that there is variance in how compelling, motivating, or appealing the ideas are (and these hypothetical ideas were developed in five minutes by one person). In practice, a team of experts would generate dozens of these problem statements after listening to and observing consumers, as well as assessing consumer data. Today, it's even possible for marketers to cocreate these problem statements with consumers through community boards, social media, or collaboration sessions. You can now imagine the breadth of ideas (and therefore the breadth in appeal and the potential to develop stronger or weaker concepts) if the problem statements were generated by a team of experts in concert with consumer insights.

Continuing with our Smartwater example, all four problem statements are not equally strong. I conducted a survey (via a convenience sample) and found that of the four problem statements, number four had the strongest appeal (i.e., greatest purchase intent). Why do you think that is? Why does that idea appeal to more bottled-water drinkers than the other three statements? The reason is that this statement addresses the full scope of the problem and what the consumer is looking for, which leads to the solution statement. Through this process, it is possible to see the difference between this scientific approach to concept development and the nonscientific approach that many firms employ.

The Solution Statement

This general process of using consumer insights to generate dozens of problem statements and then testing to determine the strongest one is consistent in the next step—identifying the best solution (i.e., consumer benefit) to the problem statement. The solution statement needs to directly connect with and solve the chosen problem statement. The clearer the linkage, the more likely that the problem statement will result in a compelling and motivating solution statement, which will help save both time and money. For example, a problem statement that ends with "I wish that I had (fill in the blank)" sets up a solution statement starting with "Introducing (fill in the blank). Now you can (solution or benefit)," which connects directly to the consumer's wishes as expressed in the problem statement. It is also important to note that the solution statement is written in the second person, as if the brand is speaking directly to the consumer. This is because the statements will be tested with actual target consumers.

In our scenario, once the problem statements are strengthened through consumer feedback (e.g., word choice evolves as consumers pick apart the specific wording through qualitative insight), and the final problem statement isdetermined via testing, the Smartwater Brand Manager needs to develop dozens of solution statements to the problem identified. Given that the "winning" problem statement given here was number four, the brand team could develop the following solution statements:

1. Introducing the new Smartwater Iceee Bottle. Now your water stays colder, providing you with that right-out-of-the-refrigerator, crisp, pure water taste.
2. Introducing the new Smartwater Iceee Bottle. Now your water stays colder longer, providing you with that right-out-of-the-refrigerator, crisp, pure water taste for hours.
3. Introducing the new Smartwater ArcticCold Bottle. Now your water stays colder for an extended period of time, so you can have great-tasting water throughout the day.
4. Introducing new Smartwater Pure Taste. Now your water stays colder longer, so you can experience PureWater taste longer.

Notice a few differences in the solution statements. First, the experts would often generate hundreds of different names to represent the concepts that they can present to consumers. While I included different names in the solution statements for the purpose of understanding, in reality, the concept identification would come first, and then the product name would be tested separately. Second, observe how word choice can potentially affect appeal. The only difference between number one and number two is the notion of "extended coldness." What sounds more compelling—colder water or water that stays colder longer? Third, in developing concepts, marketers can trademark terms that help to communicate an idea more effectively.

Notice the use of "PureWater" to describe taste in the fourth solution statement. As you can now start to see, the scientific development of a superior concept requires better consumer insight that in turn is translated into better ideas. Doing this isn't easy.

The Supporting Statement

As dozens of solution statements are identified to address the problem statement, it is important to test these ideas qualitatively and quantitatively with consumers. Once the brand team decides on the top solution statements (you can't work with 100 different solution statements, so quantitative testing is required in order to focus on the strongest ideas), it works to develop support that proves that the new brand or product can deliver on the promise made in the solution statement. Anybody can claim that water will stay colder longer, but why should the consumer believe it? Here are five possible supporting statements that the brand team could generate, addressing the solution statements in our example:

1. That's because the bottle has the new StayFreeze technology, which creates an isothermic barrier that works like a refrigerator, maintaining a cold water temperature for up to six hours.
2. That's because the bottle has the new BarrierFreeze technology, which prevents the outside temperature from warming the water for up to six hours.
3. That's because the bottle was developed by leading scientists from the Massachusetts Institute of Technology (MIT), who integrated concepts from cold fusion with Cryopak packaging technology to develop the first extended-temperature-control bottle.
4. That's because in a blind taste test, consumers rated the Smartwater Pure Taste water "cold" up to ten times longer than the leading bottled water.

5. That's because in a blind taste test, consumers gave the Smart-water Pure Taste water the highest taste rating possible.

To generate better supporting statements, marketers need to become experts on product technology and should solicit input from the scientists in R&D who can provide granularity around how a new product might work. In addition, having consumers "think out loud" and describe their experience while testing a product can be a powerful way to generate supporting statements. Doing research and talking with suppliers, industry experts, and other team members are other ways to generate novel supporting statements. To come up with option 3, for instance, I used the Bing search engine to investigate phrases such as "packaging to keep liquids cold."

This part of the concept development process can often be the most challenging because the consumer's belief in the product solution depends on proving why your solution will actually completely solve the initial problem. If a company creates a faster car, what is the marketing support that convinces the consumer that the car is in fact faster? If a company creates a safer car, what is the support for that statement? Why should consumers believe that Walt Disney World Resorts provides a superior family experience? Competitive differentiation often rests on the supporting facts used to convince consumers that the product in question is superior.

The solution statements should also be based on what *might be* possible. In this case, I made up an idea about partnering with leading scientists from MIT. Assume that the company wasn't partnering with MIT, but that it might be possible to do so in the future. If the idea tested really well, then the marketing and R&D teams could work to see whether a partnership with MIT was possible. This is where deep consumer insight and creative thinking can significantly strengthen a positioning idea that then helps lead product, promotion, and even strategic partnership development down a specific path.

Few companies do a good job of explaining the technology, process, or attributes that prove the brand can effectively deliver the solution.

Take Papa John's as an example. There are a lot of pizza companies trying to convince consumers to pick them. Papa John's says that they have better pizza, but why should consumers believe this claim? The company's answer is that Papa John's pizza is made with better and fresher ingredients. Through advertisements, the brand reinforces that the company uses real, fresh (not frozen) ingredients. Other pizza companies focus on communicating a benefit or solution that is based solely on price or on delivery service. While some consumers want cheaper pizza or faster delivery, many consumers want a better-quality pizza with fresher ingredients—a differentiated and compelling positioning concept.

While Papa John's support statement is very straightforward, a support statement can often include multiple elements to support it. For example, assume that a big problem among consumers buying new homes is that they want their home to be maintenance-free for a longer time—they don't want to have to worry about repair problems. Now assume that there is one homebuilder who has invested significant R&D resources into solving this problem. This builder has created new materials, building processes, and testing protocols to ensure a better build that is maintenance-free for longer. It would be difficult to provide one idea that could effectively support this whole solution. Instead, the marketers might want to create supporting statements that incorporate proof of better materials, processes, and testing protocols. The problem and solution statements should ideally be focused on a single idea, but part of the challenge of developing a superior support statement is that it might require more than one idea to be convincing, believable, and differentiating.

Importantly, while the proof statements are created with R&D using consumer insight, they may need to evolve once the product is developed. It is critical that the concept and product match. In the Smartwater example, if the final bottle keeps the water cold for only two hours, then the concepts need to change accordingly and be retested to ensure their appeal and interest.

Finally, while this hypothetical example was used to illustrate a line extension for an existing brand, the same process can be used to identify a white space territory for a new brand.

Key Principles of Developing a Superior Positioning Concept

While there is variance across firms in how positioning concepts are developed, there are some essential principles to keep in mind:

1. **It should be a stand-alone document.** The document should be well written and it should not require an interpreter, a translator, or any additional documents to explain it. In addition, the final document should be formatted so it can be tested with consumers (see box 2.1 for an example).

2. **It cannot be created in isolation.** Great strategic plans require "workshopping": sharing it with consumers, key partners, key employees, and key mentors to gain perspective, insight, and feedback. While the marketer is typically the ultimate decision-maker, the more insight that can be gleaned from trusted and respected colleagues, the stronger the final concept will be—and the easier it will be to "sell it in" to the broader organization.

3. **Idea generation should be expansive.** During concept creation, it's critical not to limit brainstorming or idea generation. The goal is to develop as many excellent ideas as possible, although this will also create many terrible ideas. If ideas achieve similar purchase-intent scores during the testing stage, that is a signal that the team isn't thinking broadly enough. Tremendous variation in testing will help the team understand what makes a good idea and how it differs from a bad idea.

4. **In reality, this process requires a lot of iteration.** While it would be terrific to follow a purely linear path, I've found

that this process tends to be much more iterative in practice. One might develop a great problem statement only to find that the solution statement isn't compelling. This finding would require the team to choose a different problem/solution anchor. Also, without strong support statements, the concept will not be able to achieve its full potential.

BOX 2.1
Examples of Positioning Concepts

(More Rational Positioning)

Over the years, countless products have been introduced to help you care for your clothing: new detergents, new stain removers, new fabric softeners. However, nothing has been introduced to go beyond this basic care to actually improve how you feel in your clothes, how they look on you, and how comfortable they are to wear.

Introducing New Brand X Fabric Powder! For the first time, there is a way to *improve* the look, feel, and comfort of clothes . . . so you can always look and feel your best! Just sprinkle one cup of Brand X on your clothes when you place them in the washing machine. You will be able to see and feel the difference as soon as you take them out of the dryer.

That's because the proprietary powder formula improves clothing in three ways: (1) it relaxes the fibers to make wrinkles disappear; (2) it smooths the fibers to release the tension in your clothes so they are softer and more comfortable to wear; and (3) it restores the "freshly laundered" scent of Brand X that you love.

(Less Purely Rational Positioning)*

You've always enjoyed going out and drinking with your buddies, but hate the "hoppy" aftertaste that comes with some beers. Wouldn't it be great if there were a drink that was more refreshing, but not "weak"? Unfortunately, you're forced to choose between a beer and a (not so) hard lemonade. But it shouldn't have to be that way.

Introducing Brand X! Get the crisp, refreshing taste you crave . . . in a pint glass, and not in some lightweight drink.

That's because Brand X is crafted using tradition, experience, and fruit from hundred-year-old farms that isn't too sweet. We're angry so you don't have to be.

* Thanks to the Darden School of Business's "Strategic Positioning" 2018 elective class, who created this concept. It was devised by converting Angry Orchard advertising into a positioning concept.

Summary

A skill in positioning concept development is a valuable capability, especially in mid- to senior-level marketing positions. And yet it takes a lot of practice. The better you become at generating deep consumer understanding and converting it into superior ideas, the more effective you will be across your entire professional career. The ability to understand others' problems and create effective solutions lies at the heart of being a good employee, a good CEO, a good politician, a good marketer, a good boss, and a good spouse or friend. And the best way to develop a competency is to go through the concept development process over and over again.

At some point, you will be more adept at understanding and predicting consumer responses, simply because you've created and tested hundreds of ideas. You will become more calibrated and more effective at developing superior concepts more efficiently, and you will be able to use this talent to more effectively lead your organization and support your peers and management team in creating—and communicating—superior positioning.

3

The Brand Essence Statement

> Certainly, all of the hard evidence is there for the central importance
> of the brand. . . . The intangible element of the combined market
> capitalization of the FTSE 100 companies has increased to around
> 80 percent, compared with 40 percent 20 years ago, and it is likely
> to grow even further as tangible distinctions between businesses
> become less sustainable. The brand element of that combined
> market value amounts to around 1/3 of the total, which confirms
> the brand as the single most important corporate asset.
> —RITA CLIFTON, *BRANDS AND BRANDING*[1]

MARKETING STRATEGY IS ABOUT first identifying a desired position
in the marketplace that will provide the greatest opportunity to create value for your chosen consumer target (and consequently for your
brand). Once the desired position is determined, the next step is to
begin developing a brand that can own that position if implemented
effectively. This chapter will further explore the marketing strategy
process by introducing the brand essence statement (BES), a critical
tool in helping to define the attributes of a desired brand.

To begin with, what comes to mind when you think of Nike? How
about ESPN? Or NASCAR? Or Kim Kardashian? How did Tide, over
nearly seventy years since its inception, come to stand for superior
performance on the toughest laundry problems? Why does Coca-
Cola own the idea of "refreshing" in the minds of consumers?

Over time, successful brands come to stand for something. They
carry meanings, feelings, and emotions that are captured in the hearts
and minds of consumers. These perceptions of a brand (i.e., the brand
image) affect whether consumers are interested in purchasing a product or service, how much they are willing to pay for it, and the degree

to which they are willing to share their feelings, thoughts, and recommendations with others (e.g., word of mouth and social media).

What remains elusive to many companies and marketers, however, is how to determine what the brand essence should be so that you can then implement it in such a way as to ensure that the brand image you have is the one you want. As an example of how important a brand essence is in driving overall performance, consider J. C. Penney.

J. C. Penney's leadership, in an attempt to increase profitability, changed the brand strategy, which then impacted their marketing plans. Specifically, an important element of the J.C. Penney brand experience had been the fun part of finding a deal. The firm's leaders, however, changed a core element of the brand benefit—the discount—by reducing the number and type of traditional promotions—or the fun, discount part of the brand experience. This change in the BES, which was essentially a manifestation of the positioning of the company in the market, led to an overall brand redesign. This redesign eventually failed, as consumers rejected the shift; the CEO was fired and the president left after only about 8 months in the job.[2]

The process of developing a superior BES—and then consistently delivering it—is difficult. And unfortunately, while almost all marketers work on developing, evolving, reinventing, and/or strengthening their brand's image, it can be quite challenging to do all these things well. But they can be done. Identifying the essence of a brand such that it fits with the target, can suit the current brand, and is superior to competitors requires artistry and science—artistry to create a BES and science to assess, refine, validate, and perfect it.

What Is a Brand?

A brand is "a distinguishing name and/or symbol intended to identify the goods or services of either one seller or a group of sellers, and to differentiate those goods or services from those of competitors."[3]

Think of the Nike logo (i.e., the famous swoosh), and the iconic Mercedes-Benz symbol. These brands are quickly identified by several elements, such as logos, colors, and shapes. These brands stand for something in the hearts and minds of consumers and over time have created a brand image.

The Axios Harris Poll 100 annually ranks the reputations of the most visible companies in the United States.[4] The 2019 survey of 18,228 people, designed to identify the most loved and hated companies in the country, found that the most-loved brand was Wegmans, whose consumers (called "fans") went above and beyond to espouse passion for the chain. To be deemed the most-loved brand, Wegmans went beyond merely standing for a grocery store to embody a much deeper meaning to consumers. This took a clear notion of what the company (brand) wanted to stand for, which they consistently and excellently executed over time. From logistics to products to store design to real estate locations to promotion to customer service to the in-store experience, every aspect of the company delivers their BES consistently, leading to Wegmans becoming a beloved community brand.

In contrast, near the bottom of the list were Phillip Morris, Wells Fargo, and Goldman Sachs—to put it kindly, the least-loved brands.[5] Over time, these companies have managed to acquire a negative image among the general public.[6] Everything that brands do and say ultimately contributes to how consumers perceive them (i.e., brand image) and affects consumer behavior (i.e., purchase behavior and loyalty) and ultimately firms' financial performance.[7]

What Is a Brand Image?

Brands make promises about what they can deliver to consumers. Think of Walmart as an example. Consumers see advertisements (online, in store, in circulars, on television and radio, on billboards, in print media, and so on) that tell stories about the

Walmart brand; these advertisements make promises about what the brand is and how it can provide value to consumers. Walmart's current tagline, "Save Money. Live Better," is effective in its simplicity, and it delivers on its central promise—namely, that the brand will enable consumers to save more money, which they then can use to live a better life.

But advertising is only a small part of what determines brand image. There are also the observations that consumers can make about the company. How does a news report about how much Walmart pays its average employee affect the public perception of the brand? How does information that consumers see in social media affect what they think of Walmart? How does news of a Walmart truck hitting the comedian Tracy Morgan's limousine affect what consumers think? In addition to all these ads, news stories, and other information, consumers will actually experience Walmart. What was the overall shopping experience like? Were products in stock? How competent and helpful were the employees? Were the products as cheap as consumers expected? And when store-brand products were purchased, did they live up to consumer expectations? If marketing promises one thing and the firm's actions communicate something else, consumer confusion and cognitive dissonance occur. The entire experience—judged against the promise—affects what consumers think of the brand.

Considering the previous examples of Philip Morris, Wells Fargo, and Goldman Sachs, how did they become the most-disliked companies? How has Goldman Sachs become a symbol of corporate—Wall Street—greed in the United States? Is it because of a promise that the company made but did not fulfill? Goldman Sachs barely does any traditional marketing, and yet it has acquired an undesirable image. What a brand is exists in the hearts and minds of consumers; to develop and manage a brand effectively, you start by defining the desired brand (i.e., the BES) and then implementing it consistently and effectively across all brand actions.

The Brand Essence Statement

Brands make promises to consumers, but where do these promises come from? How do brand teams decide what promise to make? This is where the BES comes in. A BES is a document, picture, video, or some other communication vehicle that captures, usually in words and visuals, the intrinsic nature and indispensable quality that make a brand unique, compelling, and meaningful to a target. It is essentially a blueprint that defines the pieces and parts of the brand and provides a guide against which to implement the brand. And it is designed to expand on the positioning concept (described in the last chapter) by converting the desired positioning territory into a brand strategy document.

Importantly, the BES goes far beyond marketing communications to describe the holistic nature of the brand—what you want your target consumers to think about it. For example, at the heart of Walmart's rational benefit (see the section entitled "How to Write a Brand Essence Statement," later in this chapter) is the notion that the brand provides the lowest prices for consumers. While this is communicated through advertising, the BES also informs companywide decision-making.

Think about how decisions related to the following business activities are informed by the BES (they are by no means an exhaustive list, but they are good places to start):

1. Logistics activities (e.g., investing in innovations that help reduce procurement and distribution costs)
2. Hiring and training activities (e.g., building a sense of thrift into employee behavior, such as taking buses to meetings instead of planes)
3. Finance activities (e.g., finding efficiencies across an entire enterprise)
4. Analyst calls (e.g., CEO statements that reaffirm the commitment to delivering products at low costs)

Even something as seemingly insignificant as the design and decor of headquarters offices should fit the BES. How might you imagine the headquarters of Walmart to look like, as opposed to that of Goldman Sachs? Walmart has a basic, functional decor that signals a commitment to low cost, whereas Goldman Sachs has an expensive decor to reflect their brand essence as a successful financial firm. In sum, the BES is much more than simply a messaging statement. It does not come *after* a product is designed but rather is created at the beginning to guide the product that should be created. It serves as a beacon, or the north star that summarizes the brand's unique positioning in the marketplace, directing and aligning all firm operations, actions, and communications. To achieve their desired brand image, an entire enterprise must be committed, through every function, geography, business unit, and person, to delivering on the brand promise.

For many firms, the development of a BES is a critical step in driving global alignment. Whether it is McDonald's, General Motors, Samsung, or Procter & Gamble, multinational firms often use BESs in both written and video-based formats to help ensure that their brands are being understood and managed consistently by their employees across the world. As such, the BES serves to unify a large, often unwieldy organization spread over multiple time zones so it can work as one entity toward the building of a single brand. Just as McDonald's wants their customers to have a similar experience in Tokyo and New York City, other companies want their brands to have a consistent image across time and place. To make this happen, McDonald's employees located in Tokyo, Prague, and New York must all have the same understanding of the brand's essence and work in a synchronous manner.

Aligning the BES with Reality

Typically, marketing leaders create the BES based on the position that they want the brand to achieve in the future (i.e., its ideal state), not where the brand is today. Just as a blueprint defines a building that is to be constructed, the BES typically defines the brand image that a marketing leader is working to develop. But while it's important to understand the future state that a marketing leader is designing to reach, it can't be divorced from today's reality. For example, if a retailer has significantly outdated store decor and its BES mentions a "superior, contemporary store design," a critical gap exists. This would be a problem because the brand positioning is out of step with reality.

As a result, it would be better to identify a BES that is more consistent with the reality that the company delivers today while developing, as part of a strategic plan (see chapter 5), a way to overcome the store design barrier.[8] The BES helps serve as an important filter when thinking through brand decisions (e.g., positioning, product, pricing, and promotion); however, it's also important to recognize that the BES is a blueprint for a brand under construction, and you need to know where you are in that building process before you make promises.

When Do Companies Create a Brand Essence Statement?

BESs are typically created after the segmentation, target definition, and positioning concept have been determined (see figure 3.1).[9] While some companies may use the BES process to help refine a brand's broader positioning, the BES is often a manifestation of the previously determined positioning.

For companies with an *umbrella brand* architecture—that is, the firm name and brand name are the same, such as with Best Buy—the BES is an expanded version of the positioning statement. It helps provide more details around the firm's positioning by outlining the rational benefits, emotional benefits, supporting attributes, and other features. For companies that have a *house of brands* architecture—that is, the firm name and the brands are different, such as with PepsiCo, which owns Pepsi, Mountain Dew, Quaker Oats, and Lay's, among other products—the BESs for the individual brands will be different from the firm's positioning statement.

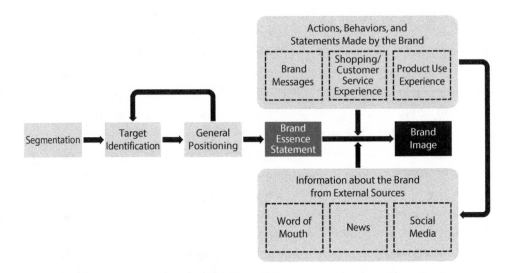

FIGURE 3.1 The brand development process
Source: Created by the author

As figure 3.1 illustrates, the role of the BES is to create a definition of the desired brand against which the company designs, develops, finances, delivers, and messages products and experiences. What affects the ultimate brand image? It is the degree to which the brand is positioned against a meaningful consumer problem and then, the brand's actions, combined with external media, news, and social media about the brand, align with the BES. Total alignment, of course, is the ultimate goal. The hope for strategic marketers is that the brand image mirrors the BES in every aspect.

The Brand Promise-Image Gap

When the brand promise and behavior do not align, issues can arise that can damage the health, image, and success of a brand. In the Axios Harris Poll 100 mentioned earlier, Comcast was listed as one of the brands that had fallen the most from 2018 to 2019 (from number 78 to number 91), being listed among the least-loved (and most-reviled) brands in the

United States.[10] Despite the fact that its advertisements promise great customer service, a simple Google search of "I hate Comcast" will result in nearly 700,000 results. For years, Comcast had a near-monopoly in the geographies in which they operated, so they were protected from the consequences of a negative brand image. But since they have had to compete for customers with firms that offer streaming content, Comcast has had quarter-after-quarter declines in the number of subscribers.[11]

This example is just one illustration of how long-term inconsistency between the BES and actions of a brand can create a negative brand image that will ultimately have detrimental business consequences.

How to Write a Brand Essence Statement

Writing a BES requires disaggregating the brand into its relevant pieces and parts to ensure that each element is articulated. For example, when you walk into a house, you experience the complete structure and have perceptions about it—how it looks, how it feels, etc. The architect of the house has a blueprint with lines, measurements, and other details that inform the construction workers on how to build the structure. But after the architecture is realized, it is your perception of the house that matters. In a similar manner, a brand is defined by how consumers perceive it—what they think and how they feel when they experience it, whether through viewing ads or shopping in a store. Brand architects (i.e., strategists) create the blueprint (i.e., the BES) with its sub-elements detailed so all the construction workers (i.e., a firm's employees) can build and deliver the brand according to the strategist's intentions. While each company has their own format, with attributes that are most relevant for their circumstances, there are four key BES elements that tend to be common across companies:

1. **Foundation:** The brand's values and personality
2. **Impact:** The benefits that the brand will provide to the consumer—both rational and emotional

3. **Support:** The proof that the brand can deliver on the rational benefits

4. **Brand essence:** The summary statement of what the brand can do for the target consumer

While some firms will have more levels and attributes that comprise the BES, these four are a good starting point from which to create a brand. Every company tends to have a different way of visualizing the BES, with most using either a pyramid or Parthenon format. A *Parthenon* format, which I will use throughout the rest of the chapter, is shown in figure 3.2 to illustrate how a brand, such as Apple, Louis Vuitton, or Fiji water, can be disaggregated into these four distinct BES elements. For examples of other types of BESs, such as the pyramid or dog-bone format, see the appendix at the end of the chapter.[12]

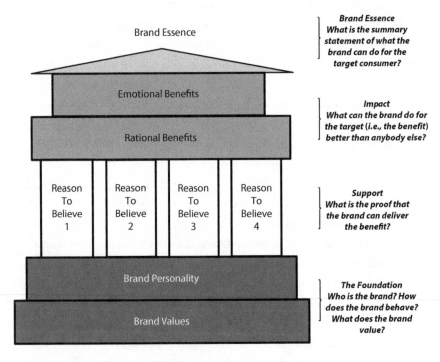

FIGURE 3.2 The Parthenon BES format
Source: Created by the author

The Foundation: Brand Values

The bottom of the Parthenon includes the brand's values and personality, or the foundation of what the brand will stand for and how it will act. The brand's values establish its principles and standards of behavior and define what is important. This is not just a set of words, as it specifically sets the boundaries of behavior. As an example, at the core of PetSmart's values are a deep commitment and concern for the well-being of pets.[13] Consequently, the founders of PetSmart created PetSmart Charities in 1994 to help ensure "a lifelong, loving home for every pet."[14] PetSmart consistently lives these values by (1) creating dog and cat adoption centers in nearly every one of their more than 1,600 stores rather than selling cats and dogs (forgoing significant revenue and profit) and (2) partnering with over 3,700 animal welfare groups across North America to help serve pets in need. The result is that roughly one of every ten dog and cat adoptions in North America is facilitated through PetSmart Charities, effectively helping over 8 million pets in need.[15] PetSmart is also the largest funder of animal welfare efforts in North America, providing $45 million in funding annually, including providing more than 214,000 spay/neuter surgeries and aiding more than 9,200 pets requiring emergency relief in 2017.

When I worked at PetSmart, the brand value of deep caring and concern transcended the charitable arm and affected everything from the company's recruiting process (how they interviewed candidates), to which employees were hired (those who demonstrated significant concern for pets), to the training process, store layout, merchandise, and so on. Interestingly, most consumers aren't aware of how deep these efforts transcend the firm because it is *not* an ad campaign—it is a set of values that the company lives every day. Even the weekly executive meeting was influenced by the brand's values, with the head of PetSmart Charities discussing key charitable initiatives and making sure that the consumer brand, PetSmart, was always connected to the charitable arm.

It cannot be overstated how important brand values are as they establish the boundaries of behavior and are embedded in actions and deeds. Just as people may say one thing and do another, an individual's—and a brand's—values are identifiable through actions, and it is important for a brand's values to resonate with consumers. For example, PetSmart cares deeply about the well-being of pets, and so does their target demographic. The two are so in sync that when PetSmart behaves according to the brand values, this connects with consumers and creates a stronger bond. As another example, if the Red Bull brand values risk-taking and living life to the fullest but the target consumer does not share the same values, then as a brand strategist, you risk creating a brand that won't be relevant or resonate with the target. I will elaborate on this later in the chapter, given the growing interest in brands focusing on communicating values rather than product-related attributes.

To work through an example, we will "reverse engineer" values by looking at a completed ad. If possible, view the Papa John's commercial found on YouTube.[16] If you don't have access, box 3.1 contains the text of the ad.

BOX 3.1
Papa John's Commercial

Visuals throughout commercial: Images of fresh ingredients (tomatoes, mushrooms, garlic, onions, etc.) being freshly cut, sliced, peeled, and shaved (e.g., slicing and grating cheese), cutting back and forth to the founder talking.

Copy in First Frame: Tomatoes go from vine to can in about six hours.

Papa John's Founder Voiceover: You expect the best, we deliver. We just believed that if we gave the consumers our best, they'd come back. That desire and fanaticism for quality has made us tick from day one. Papa John's Pizza . . . that's the kind of pizza I want to serve my family. How about you? Better Ingredients. Better Pizza. Papa John's.

Logo and tagline in Last Frame: Better Ingredients. Better Pizza. Papa John's.

As you watch the commercial, what are the values upon which you believe the brand is built? As is true in this case, it is often quite difficult to discern, because brand values aren't always clearly communicated in an ad. When this happens, leave this section of the BES blank. As we work through this process, you will notice that there are often parts of a BES that aren't clear or haven't been developed. That isn't necessarily an issue. It may just be that the brand is being developed over time. In the case of Papa John's, after reviewing a number of ads, their website, news releases, and other information, a potential set of values could be based on "family." Many of the documents mention or visualize traditional family values—mom/dad caring for children, bringing people together, etc. See figure 3.3 for a completed version of the BES for Papa John's.

Questions to ask: What are the brand's values? How do its values shape the brand's actions and behavior? And do the brand's values positively resonate with the target audience?

The Foundation: Brand Personality

Most brands have a personality, and this is a critical element of brand design. Ariel in Europe and Tide in the United States (both laundry detergents) are Procter & Gamble (P&G) brands with similar profiles, targeting a similar segment of the population. Their rational and emotional benefits are similar, but their personalities have been, historically, quite different. Tide was portrayed more like a close neighborhood friend: warm, caring, and competent when it came to household laundry. Ariel, on the other hand, came across as a little stuffy and, to some, pompous. A slight difference in the personality of the brand can affect the entire brand image. In the Papa John's commercial, if the brand were a person, how would you describe their personality? Perhaps as a friendly, warm, and health-oriented cooking expert who genuinely cares about where ingredients come from and how food is prepared.

Questions to ask: If this brand were a person, who would they be? What characteristics would you use to describe the brand (e.g., fun, homebody, adventurous, humble, self-effacing, goofy, serious, masculine, etc.)?

The Impact: Rational Benefit

The *rational benefit* is the tangible benefit that the product or service provides a consumer. What is the meaningful or relevant benefit that your brand can provide the target consumer better than your competitors? How about for Old Spice deodorant? Or Porsche? Products and services are purchased primarily to solve a consumer problem, which could be functional or utilitarian, such as wanting a car with better gas mileage or a shampoo that will make hair softer and shinier. Likewise, that problem could be emotional, such as making a consumer feel smarter, more confident, more successful, or more beautiful (we'll look at emotional benefits more in the section entitled "Impact: Emotional Benefit," later in this chapter).

In the context of understanding rational benefits, consider the Papa John's ad again. Because you would assume that the commercial was created from a BES, it is a helpful task to reverse engineer the BES (i.e., write a BES based on the company's marketing communications). In this case, the commercial communicates that the rational benefit of choosing Papa John's is better pizza by overtly communicating the words "better pizza." The commercial doesn't say "good pizza" or "OK pizza." It specifically says "better pizza," and it even implies "the best pizza" (e.g., "you expect the best, we deliver"). Consequently, the tangible, rational benefit that the consumer receives from eating Papa John's Pizza is "better pizza." Of note, many brands don't have (and therefore don't communicate) a rational benefit. This often happens in categories where there are not tangible, measurable features, such as wine or clothing.

Question to ask: What is the tangible (i.e., measurable, observable, definable) benefit that this brand will deliver for the target customer?

The Impact: Emotional Benefit

The rational benefit of a brand often connects to a consumer's intellect (i.e, their brain), while the emotional side connects to the heart. Why would a mom who is feeding her family pizza care about choosing Papa John's over another brand? How does it make it her feel? This benefit is rarely overtly communicated in a commercial. It is sometimes implied in the execution. In the Papa John's commercial, for instance, the founder, in chef's gear, says: "That's the kind of pizza I want to feed my family. How about you?" He is essentially suggesting that parents (caregivers) who care about their families will want to feed them only the best. So how might a mom or dad feel? They might feel like great parents who can take pride in providing their family with a high-quality dinner that they know they will love.

Similarly, why might a mom or dad care about using a laundry detergent whose rational benefit statement is "Provides the best value-oriented cleaning for parents on a budget"? The answer lies in the emotional benefit. In the case of the laundry detergent, the emotional benefit might be that the caregiver was smart because they didn't waste money on overpriced laundry detergent. The emotional benefit is often a key way of distinguishing brands. In a number of categories, there is often a brand that ladders up to an emotional benefit centered on being smart (e.g., Luvs, Buick) or on providing the best care for the family (e.g., Pampers, Subaru).

Questions to ask: So what? Why do target consumers care about the rational benefit that your product (or service) offers? What does this mean for them on an intangible—or emotional—level?

The Support: Reasons to Believe

Between the brand's foundation and its rational and emotional benefits are the pillars of support—the reasons to believe or "proof points" discussed in chapter 2. Any pizza company can say "better pizza," but today's consumers are skeptical. Why should they believe that Papa John's pizza is better than anybody else's? Providing this support is absolutely critical. Without demonstrating the proof of a brand's ability to deliver the benefit promised, consumers may not believe the promise. In the case of the Papa John's commercial, the visuals and copy work together to demonstrate that the company uses only ingredients that are fresh and hand-cut to make its pizza better than that of the competition, effectively supporting their promise. You'll notice in this case that there is only one pillar of support. A single, compelling reason to believe is more valuable than two or more weaker proof points.

But many marketers overlook the criticality of providing both accurate and convincing support that the brand can deliver the promised benefit. For example, during my time as a professor at the University of Virginia's Darden School of Business, I worked with the marketing team who led an exercise to understand why the Master's of Business Administration (MBA) program had been rated, nine years in a row, as "the world's best teaching experience" by the *Economist*.[17] In this case, "the world's best teaching experience" could be used as a rational benefit. If so, it should be reframed so that it is from the perspective of the student. The "best teaching experience" is from the perspective of the professor or the school; instead, it should identify how the "best teaching experience" benefits the target (i.e., the prospective student) "Darden provides the world's best learning and growth experience." If this is the rational benefit, then what are the best proof points to confirm that Darden can deliver this benefit? In this case, the nine-year ranking by the *Economist* is one potential proof point. It is an external source of empirical evidence that the Darden brand delivers on the rational benefit.

Without any evidence or proof, the rational benefit simply becomes an unfounded claim. Trust lies at the heart of successful brands. The strongest brands don't make promises they can't keep or state benefits they can't deliver. If you are creating, evolving, or strengthening a brand, one of the most important issues is to ensure that the rational benefit and support are connected, are compelling, resonate convincingly with the consumer—and that the product, service, or experience can deliver.

Questions to ask: What is the proof that this brand can deliver on the rational benefit promise made? What evidence do you have that will convince the target consumer that this brand can effectively deliver on the promise?

Brand Essence

The pinnacle of the Parthenon-based BES is the *essence*—a summary of the brand that defines what the strategists want the brand to be in the mind and heart of the target consumer. This, then, becomes a summary statement that includes all four aspects that define the brand: (1) who the target consumer is, (2) the frame of reference for the brand, (3) the benefits that the brand provides the consumer, and (4) the evidence for the promised benefit.

In the context of the Papa John's commercial, the brand essence would be something like, "To parents concerned about the quality of food their family eats, Papa John's creates better pizza so that you can be confident that you are providing the best food for your family." First, you will notice that this statement is written in the second person. It is written as if the company is talking directly to the consumer. This makes the brand more personal and helps ensure that the strategists are more connected to the consumer. Second, notice that the rational benefit leads right into the emotional benefit. The two are directly connected. Finally, this is the first place where the target consumer is defined and connected to the design of the brand. In total, the brand essence serves as a short summary of what the brand will strive to do and be for the consumer.

Questions to ask: What is the essence of the brand—or a short summary of what the brand will do for the target consumer?

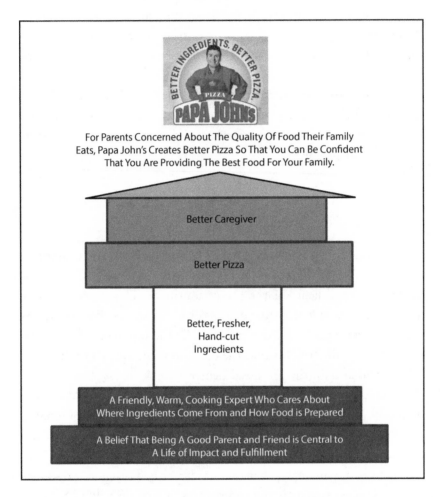

For Parents Concerned About The Quality Of Food Their Family Eats, Papa John's Creates Better Pizza So That You Can Be Confident That You Are Providing The Best Food For Your Family.

Better Caregiver

Better Pizza

Better, Fresher, Hand-cut Ingredients

A Friendly, Warm, Cooking Expert Who Cares About Where Ingredients Come From and How Food is Prepared

A Belief That Being A Good Parent and Friend is Central to A Life of Impact and Fulfillment

FIGURE 3.3 Example of BES for Papa John's (based on ad)

One More Example: Bounty

Bounty—the "thicker, quicker picker-upper"—is a brand that has done an excellent job of having a clear and consistent brand strategy over time. If you place ten marketing experts in a room who know how to identify brand strategy from an ad, almost all will quickly see the exact same strategy. This is a sign of a well-executed brand strategy—no

FIGURE 3.4 A Bounty ad
Source: Bounty, used with permission

ambiguity and no guesswork. In addition to having communications that clearly articulate the strategy, the brand has had essentially the same strategy over time. Take a look at the ad in figure 3.4. Can you identify each of the elements of the BES?

The rational benefit communicated in this ad is that Bounty is more absorbent so you can use fewer sheets. The emotional benefit is unclear. That's OK, though. Not all ads have emotional benefits. Many of Bounty's television commercials offer clearer emotional benefits—Bounty is a better, more absorbent paper towel (rational benefit), enabling parents to let their kids be kids, to explore without worrying about spills. The rational benefit is one of providing reassurance that Bounty will take care of spills, which ladders up to allowing parents to let their kids play without having to worry. This in turn ladders up to enabling parents to be better parents. What is the proof of the rational benefit? The copy indicates that Bounty has two times the absorbency of the leading ordinary brand of paper towel. The visual is even stronger, as it illustrates that one sheet of Bounty is still intact, while two sheets of the "leading ordinary brand" get saturated and ripped.

Step back and consider this approach. Is it a strong strategy to communicate superior absorbency? To ladder this up (in many of their ads) to enabling parents to be better parents? Is the logic compelling? It's one thing to say that Bounty towels offer better absorbency—but do these ads effectively and convincingly prove that they do this?

Bounty is an exemplar in terms of having created an effective and superior position (better absorbency), communicating the benefit in easy-to-understand terms, providing compelling evidence (visually and in copy) that supports the position, and connecting it to something that matters for their target. What do you think matters most to people who buy paper towels? Probably that it works—absorbency. In this case, Bounty's essence is helping parents become better parents by freeing them from worry so that their kids can play, explore, and grow. And that seems like a pretty important—and valuable—brand purpose.

Points to Consider When Writing a Brand Essence Statement

There are three key points that are important to remember when writing a BES and when reverse engineering competitive BESs.

1. **Not all brands design to a complete BES**: For example, when Walmart originally advertised their brand, it focused solely

on the reasons to believe—low (or at least lower) prices. They communicated that singular message over and over and ensured that the in-store experience (e.g., signage, store decor, and pricing) reinforced this message. Once established, Walmart evolved their messaging to communicate both the rational benefit (saves you money) and the emotional benefit (so you can live better).

2. **If you focus on the emotional benefit and ignore the rational benefit, the brand is vulnerable to attack:** The foundation of a brand is its rational reason for existence. Those brands that own the most important category benefit (e.g., cleaning clothes for laundry detergent; whitening teeth for toothpaste; refreshing for soda; low price for mass discounters; best-tasting food; and best clothing designs) typically have the largest market share, holding everything else equal. Why? Rational benefits matter because consumers are purchasing many products and services to meet specific needs. Whichever company best convinces consumers that it can solve that problem or fulfill that need will win.

   While some prefer to focus on the emotional benefit, the bread and butter for most brands is their rational promise and ability to prove that they can provide a meaningful benefit to their target consumer better than competitors. Consider the "Mac versus PC" commercials crafted by Apple and aired in the early 2000s. The campaign was a humorous, personality-driven, side-by-side demonstration of the rational benefits (e.g., security) of a Mac versus a PC. Apple understood that consumers wanted to buy something that was superior on some important dimension (e.g., design, speed, quality, or security).

3. **BESs will evolve over time:** As a brand grows and becomes more established in the market, it is common for brands to adjust the BES to stay relevant and interesting for the target consumer. Grey Goose vodka, for example, quickly pivoted

toward the emotional benefit once the rational benefit was established. Jif peanut butter also originally focused on the rational benefit—communicating how they used superior-quality peanuts for their peanut butter. Jif ultimately added the emotional benefit that the brand was for moms who cared about providing their family with the best ("Choosy moms choose Jif").

The Cost of Failing to Quantitatively Test a Brand Essence Statement

Even though the importance of determining a brand essence is clear, companies often hire agencies and consulting firms to create BESs, outsourcing one of the most critical aspects of business—the strategic positioning and design of their brands. Unfortunately, not all marketers or advertising agencies use quantitative testing to (1) ascertain what attributes of a brand really matter to the consumer; (2) measure how different brands deliver on the most important attributes (to identify unmet needs)—and how brands compare to one another; (3) understand what the brand stands for in the minds of current customers and prospects who choose not to purchase (i.e., brand strengths and barriers); and (4) measure how compelling and motivating the BES is relative to consumer needs and competitors' BESs.

Without quantitative insight, a marketer is unable to assess whether the BES is superior or inferior to those of competitors. If the BES design is outsourced, lack of empirical support means that the decision regarding the brand's positioning (in this case anchored in the BES) is based on outside representatives who may not have the same depth of understanding as those in the company. It isn't prudent for brand marketers to risk the business by failing to quantitatively validate the BES (i.e., ensuring it is superior to competitors and will meet target consumers' needs). Unfortunately, the reliance on a subjective assessment made by some marketers, agencies, and consulting firms can easily lead down the wrong branding path.

To have confidence that your BES will help strengthen your brand's position in the marketplace, use quantitative research to answer the following questions:

1. **What category attributes matter most to your target consumer (and which don't)?** It may be useful to generate a list of possible category attributes via qualitative interviews, secondary research (e.g., analysis of comments on social media), and preliminary surveys.

2. **How does your brand—and your primary competitors' brands—deliver on each of these important category attributes?** Are you judged by consumers as the best? This affects whether you would want to attempt to own these attributes. For example, throughout the 1980s and 1990s, Target was just another mass discounter, along with Zayre, Walmart, Venture, Kmart, and others. By the early 2000s, however, it had leapfrogged Kmart to become the second largest, behind Walmart. The most important attribute for mass discounters had historically been low prices, and Target knew that it couldn't compete with Walmart on this specific rational attribute.[18] But an important and untapped attribute that a segment of more affluent mass shoppers wanted was "discount chic," or affordable designer merchandise. None of the mass discounters were doing a good job of delivering on this attribute, and Target believed that it could pivot and shift the positioning and the BES until they ultimately owned it.

3. **Do you have the ability to effectively deliver on any of the attributes?** As this example illustrates, Target didn't believe that they could outperform Walmart on low prices, so they had to stake out another territory. They believed that they could transform their store experience, marketing, merchandise, hiring, training, advertising, and operations to effectively satisfy this novel and unmet need for discount chic.

4. **What is the purchase intent of your desired BES relative to your competitors?** If your stated positioning (as manifested through your BES) is inferior to those of your peers, holding all else equal, your actual brand image will be inferior to theirs.

The Shift in BES Prioritization over Time and a Final Word on Values-Based Marketing

At a macro level, there have been periods where marketers have emphasized various elements of the BES. During the print-dominant era of advertising, rational brand messaging was often the priority. For instance, a Dove ad from 1964 showed a side-by-side comparison of Dove and "soap," proving that it was milder (the rational benefit) than any soap.[19] During this period, advertising agencies often focused on prioritizing messages that communicated the rational benefit and reasons to believe. Print ads at this time were often dominated by copy waxing poetic about the tangible benefit that the brand could provide to the consumer.

In a 1979 Apple ad, the content was focused on educating consumers about what a computer was, why consumers should want one, and how to get one.[20] It was a copy-intensive approach to educating consumers and logically communicating the benefit of purchasing an Apple computer.

By the 1990s, however, there was a growing belief that brands had to go beyond the rational benefit to connect with consumers on an emotional level. As Kevin Roberts, the former CEO of Saatchi and Saatchi, wrote in his book *Lovemarks*:

> By the 1990s, it was clear that we were living in the Attention Economy. There were thousands of TV channels, movies, radio stations, newspapers, and magazines. Millions of websites. Billions of phone calls, faxes, and e-mails. And right through all of it, new product launches and new improved product-line extensions and ads struggling to be heard. Too much information! People are overwhelmed

by the choices they face. Forget the Information Economy. Human attention has become our principal currency.[21]

With the world's largest and most respected creators of advertising leading the way, brand communication began to focus on grabbing attention through visuals designed to drive emotion. The consequence? Brands often deprioritized and in many cases ignored the benefits (and accompanying support) that they could provide the consumer. A 1999 Absolut print ad is an example.[22]

Continuing into the 2000s, an example from Lego is noteworthy for its simplicity.[23] In this case, other than the logo, there is no copy. The pendulum had shifted to emphasize a visual method for trying to communicate the brand. When I teach executive groups how to reverse engineer brand strategy, I often put up a purely visual ad and ask each individual to identify the BES elements. We then compare our observations. Invariably, in both the Absolut ad and, to a lesser degree, the Lego one, there are nearly as many different interpretations of the BESs as there are executive participants. I then show them copy-heavy ads from an earlier era, which typically cause most students to agree on the BESs. I then ask them if it matters. Does it matter whether your target consumer, after having engaged with your brand for some time, can reliably identify your central message? Of course, the executives will say yes. The trade-off is clear. Highly visual ads can drive attention but may fail to educate, persuade, or change minds, beliefs, or behaviors.

While the shift from rational benefit communication has continued, driven by both a belief that there is too much information and the desire to ensure ads can break through the clutter, there is a new movement that focuses on the prioritization of brand values rather than just engaging the consumer with visually arresting and simple ads. Precipitated by a desire for brands to have greater social responsibility, as well as growing evidence that consumers want brands to stand for something, more and more brands are ignoring the impact and support elements of the BES when communicating these values-based messages. Recent research suggests that seven in ten consumers believe that companies have an obligation to improve issues that may not be relevant to the business.[24] In the same study, 87 percent of consumers said they'd specifically buy from a company if they advocated an issue the consumers cared about.

Armed with such evidence, brand after brand has shifted to focusing on values-based messages to appeal to this new generation of consumers. For example, Dove introduced the "Campaign for Real Beauty,"[25] designed to challenge the advertising world's view of beauty by showcasing and championing real women. This campaign was considered a success by all measures—except for one key element. Unilever, the parent company of Dove, also owned Axe, a brand that some argued objectified women and created images of unattainable beauty. An *Adweek* article highlighting the hypocrisy chronicled that an organization began a letter-writing campaign aimed at Unilever's CEO at the time, Patrick Cescau, claiming that Axe "epitomizes the sexist and degrading marketing that can undermine girls' healthy development."[26]

When marketers make values the central message rather than other attributes associated with a brand, the cost of not "walking the talk" can be significant. In 2017, Audi ran a Super Bowl ad about gender pay inequality. The ad caused controversy, with some asking what Audi (or any car company) had to do with gender pay inequality and others taking the cynical view that Audi didn't really care about it—they were trying to coopt a societal issue to sell cars.[27]

There are five factors that marketers should consider before choosing to elevate values and deprioritize other BES elements:

1. If you stand for values, you'd better stand for the "right" ones. While most consumers say that they will buy from a company who shares their values, most (76 percent) also say that they will boycott a company that promotes values they don't share.[28] In other words, if a brand takes a stand on a controversial issue, it is likely to have consumers who agree and disagree with the position. Look at the consequences of Starbuck's "Race Together" campaign, in which the company wanted to inspire "conversation starters" about race. It drew such ire by the media and the public that Starbucks had to abruptly end the effort. For example, consider headlines like "Starbucks Solves Racism—One Macchiato at a Time," and "Can Starbucks Fix Racism with a Message on a Cup?" and tweets that highlighted the hypocrisy; Twitter user @NewaHailu tweeted, "Starbucks pays Ethiopian farmers pennies for coffee beans. They turn around and charge $10 for grande latte." Beyond the potential for brand damage, what was the cost associated with designing, developing, implementing, and then cancelling the effort?

Also, consider Nike's use of the National Football League (NFL) quarterback Colin Kaepernick in an ad. To some, Kaepernick stood for being patriotic (a uniquely American principle) and standing (or kneeling, as he did during the national anthem before football games) for social injustice. Others viewed Kaepernick as anti-American and unpatriotic. When Nike chose to align its brand with Kaepernick, those who saw him positively bought more merchandise, but those who didn't not only boycotted, but in some cases burned Nike products. The challenge is that Nike had consumers on both sides of the issue, and by taking a stand, they risked alienating a likely nontrivial group of consumers. For marketing strategists, it's critical to be the "consumer's advocate" and build brands in a way that strengthens the consumer-brand relationship over time—*even when brand strategists may not have the same beliefs or values as their consumers or the brands that they are responsible for stewarding.* In other words, promoting values is a high-risk tightrope act that should not be taken lightly. Consumers want brands to espouse the right values—and "right" depends on the consumer.

2. What happens when a lot of brands focus on values? Dove was one of the brands that started this movement, but others were quick to follow. When Audi talks about gender pay inequality, Starbucks talks about race, Nike opines on social injustice, Always informs us that the statement "like a girl" is demeaning, Pepsi's Kendall Jenner ad promotes unification, Gillette talks about toxic masculinity, and so on, what impact does this have on consumers? When many brands promote values, what is the consequence? When a car company creates a gender pay inequality ad for the Super Bowl, but there is nothing else that suggests that they care about the topic (i.e., ads, public relations, actions, support, etc.), does this lead consumers to become more cynical over time? If brands don't live up to the values they espouse, how will this affect consumer trust in brands and marketing? And if many brands talk about values, does doing so then become less differentiating and compelling? Does it numb consumers? As I sit here typing, I see dog toys, a remote control, a lamp, rugs, blankets, a phone, paper clips, Sharpie pens, paper, etc. Must all these brands communicate values that often have nothing to do with the benefits that their products offer? Think back to the Bounty example. Why is providing a better product that enables parents to feel more comfortable letting their kids play not sufficient? Or is it?

3. Values are demonstrated through deeds, not words. Authenticity and veracity are the mechanisms through which brands create trust. Unfortunately, many of these values-promoting efforts appear to be a one-off attempt to coopt a hot topic. Brand strategists may be well intentioned, but that doesn't matter to consumers. Values emanate from what people do, not what they say. And the same goes for brands. It isn't a logo, a tagline, an advertisement, a message on a cup, or a voiceover in an ad that matters. It requires much deeper, sustained behavior that is done for the sake of doing it rather than for the glory of having said it. PetSmart has never fully taken advantage of or promoted all that they do for pets. They live their values, and on occasion, they promote PetSmart charity events (e.g., adoption weekends).

In contrast, after watching Audi's gender pay inequality ad, I decided to investigate the degree to which Audi actually behaves in concert with their espoused value. I looked at their board of directors and management team—nearly all men. I searched for any press releases or articles that mentioned their commitment to gender pay inequality. I visited an Audi dealership and talked to the manager about his knowledge of their efforts. I could not find any significant evidence that Audi's behaviors and actions were centered on gender pay equality. It appeared to be an advertisement—nothing more. Of note, I wrote about this in *Forbes* and was contacted by an Audi representative who indicated that the company has since added a number of initiatives to address gender pay inequality. This is terrific, but at a minimum, advertising good deeds should come after having lived them consistently for some time. The consequence of being exposed for exploiting values that matter to your consumer but are not the basis upon which you've built the brand is significant. It not only can cause damage to your own brand, but also continues to reinforce a belief that marketers are dishonest and manipulative.

4. **Marketers serve brands and the consumer—not the other way around.** I've had a number of conversations over the past few months with C-level executives who are worried that marketers are hijacking brands to serve their own needs and their own purposes. As an example, a marketer at a top-tier company created an ad that admonished consumers who didn't recycle. The problem, according to an executive at the firm, was that both the firm and brand believed in inclusion. Using an ad to lecture or scold customers was not consistent with the brand strategy. Why did the brand manager do this? Because he or she believed deeply that more consumers should recycle, and so they used the brand to communicate their own message. At senior levels of firms, activism that promotes using the firm or brands to serve the purposes of marketers (and other employees) is problematic. As marketers, we serve the consumer, and the brand, *and* the firm. And, marketers are the champions of the consumer—all of the consumers.

5. **Lastly—and this is from a purely strategic perspective—a prioritization of values to the exclusion of other BES elements leaves the brand vulnerable.** In an exercise that I use with executives, I have them take on the role of brand manager at Olay and ask them to develop ways to compete with Dove after the launch of the "Campaign for Real Beauty" using the BES outline. The answer is to throw as much energy as possible at the reason that women buy skin care products. Zig when Dove zags. While Dove focuses on the definition of beauty, there is a large segment of women who still care about finding a product that makes their skin look younger and feel healthier. This is exactly what Olay has done. While Dove focused on values, Olay concentrated on how their products can help solve key skin problems and challenges. A

recent ad solely focused on rational benefits and the reasons to believe; the title was: "The #1 New Skincare Product in 2018."[29]

To make this point more vivid, I share a confidential conversation with the CEO of a large, multinational food company. The CEO indicated that the company had been focused on communicating values and social issues on one of its flagship brands for years. The consequence was market share erosion. The company was, he said, "going back to basics" to focus on reminding consumers of the taste-related attributes of their products rather than relying on their social values. They learned that what consumers cared most about in a food product was, not surprisingly, taste.

The marketing pendulum swings. Right now, there is a desire to focus on brand values, purpose, and conquering issues that are often unrelated to the problems that consumers want brands to solve. When brand strategists focus on only one element of the BES and ignore others—for example, the rational benefit and reasons to believe—they leave the brand vulnerable to attack by competitors who focus on what matters most to the greatest number of consumers. And that, unsurprisingly, is usually associated with the problem that they are purchasing the product to solve. Consumers buy Tide to get their clothes clean; Gillette to provide a clean, smooth, comfortable shave; Bounty to absorb spills; Coke to be refreshed; Ben & Jerry's to indulge themselves in decadent flavors; and so on. They shop at Walmart to save money and at Amazon for convenience. Over time, I believe that we'll see a shift toward a middle ground as marketers realize what the CEO of the food company did—that ignoring the primary reason that consumers purchase your products leaves you vulnerable to competitive attack.

Summary

This chapter has introduced and defined the BES, a tool that strategic marketers use as a blueprint for creating and managing a brand.

Developing a superior BES requires a combination of artistry (to fully understand and tap into the needs of the consumer) and science (to ensure that your design is as strong as it can be and is validated through quantitative testing). It is not an easy process, but it is critical if you wish to develop a brand that stands out from the crowd, generates interest, and creates superior business results.

Marketers tend to make the mistake of focusing on particular elements of the BES to the exclusion of other important elements. The goal for marketing strategists is to consistently strengthen the brand, reducing the likelihood of a successful competitive attack. This means fortifying all elements of the BES and effectively delivering the strategy.

Appendix

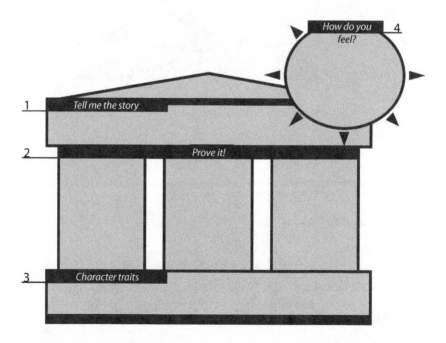

FIGURE AP 3.1 Parthenon format

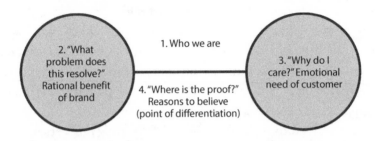

FIGURE AP 3.2 Dogbone format
Source: All figures created by author.

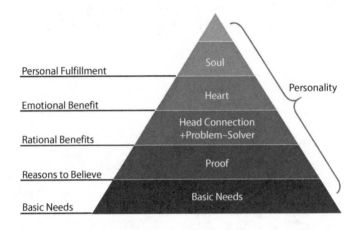

FIGURE AP 3.3 Pyramid format

FIGURE AP 3.4 Example of pyramid format: Papa John's

4

Strategy Map Types

Imagine that you are a general taking your troops into foreign territory. Obviously, you would need detailed maps showing the important towns and villages, the surrounding landscape, key structures like bridges and tunnels, and the roads and highways that traverse the region. Without such information, you couldn't communicate your campaign strategy to your field officers and the rest of your troops. . . . Organizations need tools for communicating both their strategy and the processes and systems that will help them implement that strategy.

—ROBERT S. KAPLAN AND DAVID P. NORTON[1]

IDENTIFYING A DESIRED POSITION and creating a brand essence statement (BES) that can ensure that the brand achieves that desired position is not enough. It doesn't mean anything unless it is adopted and implemented throughout your company. The next step is to effectively communicate the desired position and the BES so that the balance of the organization is clear, aligned, and committed to delivering the strategic direction. But just as with the positioning concept and BES tools described in previous chapters, finding a way to communicate in a compelling and effective manner can be difficult.

Consider the following scenario. Imagine making a presentation to a board of directors for the first time. What is the best way to distill your understanding of the business into a few, short, simple-to-understand Microsoft PowerPoint slides? The first time I presented to a board, this was the challenge—conveying in a few slides what I had digested by looking at hundreds of pages of data and reports. To influence and communicate effectively, I relied heavily on *strategy maps*, or tools that enable marketers to communicate a complex topic in a more digestible fashion via a visual that identifies and situates key strategic variables (e.g., brands, attributes, and positions), often relative to rivals, on important dimensions. For example, in one board meeting, I was trying to help the board members understand competitive positioning relative to consumer needs. A useful way to visualize this was to identify consumer needs by key demographic variables and then placing all the key brands on the map based on which demographic group and need they primarily served. This helped the board understand the key marketplace opportunity and why I was recommending particular strategies to drive growth.

This chapter is designed to foster an introductory understanding of what strategy maps are, how they are used by marketers, and some popular examples. There is no one right type of strategy map. Consequently, this discussion will provide myriad examples to expand your thinking about what strategy maps can be, what they look like, and how they can be used. Whether you are a brand manager, marketing director, consultant, general manager, or chief marketing officer (CMO), strategy maps can help you develop and communicate your marketing strategy.

Strategy Maps: What They Are and How They Are Used

Marketers use strategy maps to give a visual, fast, and easy-to-comprehend overview of the corporation, its brands, its customers, and/or the competition. Their function is to help provide a clearer understanding of a strategic issue and/or help communicate this to key constituents, such as peers, clients, the CEO, or the board of directors. Often, strategy maps can help provide insight into one of the following questions:

- Where are we as a brand/company today?
- Where are we going in the future?
- How do we plan to get there?

Teaching both executive and residential MBA students, I've noticed that businesspeople appreciate strategy maps and frameworks. When I teach core marketing, I regularly provide frameworks that help simplify concepts such as (1) the consumer decision-making process, (2) which features and benefits to prioritize (and when), (3) types of innovation, and (4) market- versus product-oriented strategic approaches. In job interviews, company recruiters request that prospective employees provide their point of view on what attributes are characteristics of stronger (versus weaker) brands, sources of growth, and other issues. These technical and case questions often require a simple way of explaining a complex answer. In my elective, students are required to create their own strategy maps to communicate a desired position for a new-to-the-world brand. I explain that they have consumed a steady diet of these tools, and they already know how helpful they are in making sense of the world. In the future, they will be hired to create these strategy maps (especially those going into consulting). They will need to take everything they know about their business and use simple tools such as strategy maps to help others quickly gain understanding. The earlier that they begin observing good (and bad) uses of strategy maps and practice creating them, the better off they will be. I frankly didn't start doing this until later in my career and I wish I had begun practicing much earlier.

The reason that these maps are valuable is because CMOs uniquely sit at the intersection of the external marketplace, the internal functions, and the C-suite. They are charged with making sense of a complex world—including consumers, competitors, and channel partners—and integrating this insight with knowledge about the firm's and brand's capabilities. By using strategy maps to synthesize and communicate, CMOs assist the C-suite in making strategic decisions that propel the company forward. Thus, strategy maps are comprehension and communication tools that can help drive better understanding, alignment, and decision-making.

An Organizing Framework for the Various Types of Strategy Maps

Although there are a number of types of strategy maps that marketers can use, most are used to provide insight into one or a combination of the following areas: (1) internal brand portfolio and resource management, (2) consumer perspectives and preferences, and (3) competitive market dynamics. These three categories and some popular examples of strategy maps are described next.

Strategy Map Type 1: Internal Brand Portfolio and Resource Management

Strategy maps are often used to understand and prioritize resources. In a conversation with a marketing-experienced board member, he indicated that at each company where he serves as a board member, he requests that the management team develop a strategy map that visualizes short- and long-term priorities by business unit (or brand, depending on the company). He indicated that boards can sometimes be focused on the short term, and this type of map forces the board to engage in resource allocation over both a short- and a long-term horizon. In this case, the board member uses the map to draw attention to strategic prioritization and resource allocation over different time horizons. See table 4.1 for a marketing version of this type of map. A popular example of this type of strategy map is the BCG matrix, which enables marketers to plot brands according to market share and market growth.

Strategy Map Type 2: Consumer Perspectives and Preferences

A common type of strategy map used by marketers, consultants, and researchers visualizes consumer perspectives, insights, preferences,

TABLE 4.1

Example of a marketing resource allocation map

	Time Horizon Impact		
	<1 year	1-3 years	3+ years
Brand			
Product			
Promotion			
Testing			
Training and Development			
Other			

Marketing Investment Priorities

To complete the map, a number of different types of information can be used in the specific cells. For example: dollars, percentage of investment, or even color coding (e.g., green means the highest percentage of investment, red the lowest, and yellow moderate levels of invesment).

To complete this map, various types of information can be used in the different cells, such as dollars, percentage of investment, or even color coding (e.g., green indicates the highest level of investment, red the lowest, and yellow moderate levels of investment).

needs, and other aspects. As an example, perceptual maps help marketers understand how consumers perceive a brand relative to key competitors on important attributes. The difficulty in creating a useful map is identifying the key attributes to compare. The example of a perceptual map shown in figure 4.1 graphically illustrates how various brands in the automotive industry are perceived on different attributes. To develop the map, key questions you'd want to ask include:

- How did you choose the attribute dimensions (i.e., conservative, sporty, and so on)?
- Why are these the right dimensions to use to compare brands?
- How did you determine where to place the brands (i.e., what research methodology was used), and how are you confident that this is the most appropriate methodology?

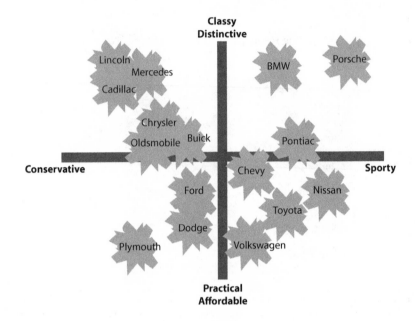

FIGURE 4.1 A perceptual map of the automotive industry
Source: Wikimedia Commons

As you can see, the rigor with which the framework is developed and the research conducted will determine whether the strategy map is useful and effective, or potentially misleading.

Strategy Map Type 3: Competitive Market Dynamics

Perfect strategies are not called for. What counts is performance relative to that of the competition.[2]

The third type of strategy map helps indicate your brand's position relative to competitors based on a specific set of parameters that are typically not grounded in consumer insight, but rather on some other relevant variables. For example, in the strategy map in figure 4.2, retail

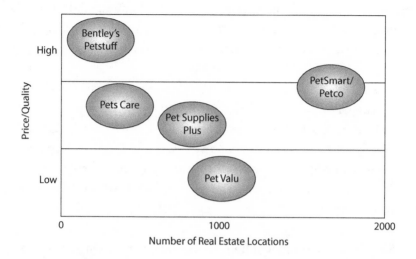

FIGURE 4.2 Retail chain strategy map
Source: Ajit Kumar (2013), "Analyzing a Company's External Environment," Slideshare, (https://www.slideshare.net/AjitKumar84/chap003-analysing-external-envrnmt (Slide 49)

chains are plotted based on empirical, observable data that includes price/quality and geographic coverage. Another practical example includes mapping product portfolio offerings (i.e., assortment), store locations, or marketing spending relative to competitors.

Strategy Maps: The Process

As with many of the processes discussed in this book so far, the strategy map development process will vary based on a number of factors, such as the objective, the nature of your business, and your data. Here is a set of steps that can provide guidance as you develop your own maps.

Step 1: Define the purpose. Before you begin, it's important to understand why you want a strategy map and how you will use it. Is it a communication tool designed to help make sense of a complex issue? A sales tool designed to sell in a recommendation? Or a simplifying matrix designed to help your team make a decision? Just as a carpenter starts with the problem to be solved and then identifies the appropriate tool to use, the marketing strategist begins by identifying the objective and works backward to design the best strategy map.

Example: Assume that you are the marketing director for Heinz Ketchup, and you are trying to identify the next flavor of ketchup to launch. You have tested two new flavors: honey ranch ketchup and chipotle ketchup. Your objective is to create a strategy map that helps you understand consumer preferences by demographic target so that you can decide which flavor would be best to launch, and then use the map to help management understand your rationale.

Step 2: Develop the wireframe (i.e., framework). Once you understand the objective, need, and purpose of the strategy map, you will start to develop a framework of the map, or the key information needed to reach the objective. It is likely that several types of information could be useful. It is a helpful exercise when you start developing the map to identify many of the ways to achieve the objective because some may be more effective than others. Figure 4.3 gives an example of what a strategy map wireframe could look like.

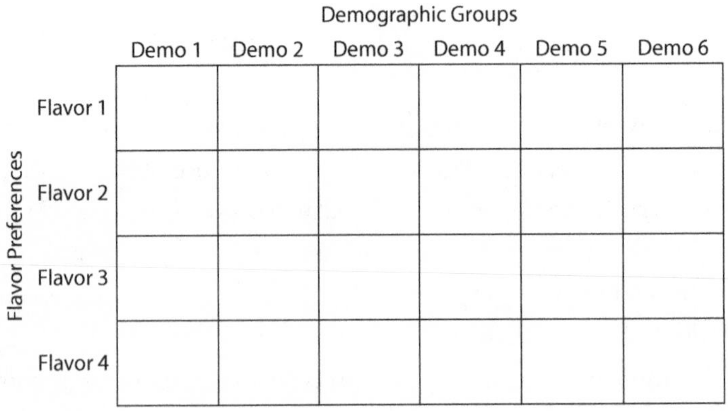

FIGURE 4.3 Strategy map wireframe

Once you identify the information, decide how it will be placed in a visual way (i.e., axes). Assume that as Heinz's marketing director, you decide to identify and communicate all flavor preferences by demography. To visualize this, start by developing a wireframe of the map. In this case, you decide that the *y*-axis will list all the currently marketed and prospective flavors (i.e., those not yet developed) that you have market research data regarding consumer preferences, and the *x*-axis will include the various key consumer demographic groups.

Step 3: Fill in the wireframe and complete the strategy map. Now that the framework is outlined, you will use the market research data to complete the map by identifying the flavors, the demographic groups, and importantly, some measure of consumer preference (e.g., market share, blind test ratings, etc.) for each. Given the original objective, this strategy map needs to include consumer preference data to provide insight on the relative importance of each flavor. In figure 4.4, the shaded boxes represent a flavor that is already in market, while the white represents a flavor that is being considered for launch. The numbers shown are the consumer preference ratings for each flavor,

Flavor Preferences	Demo 1 (15%)	Demo 2 (20%)	Demo 3 (33%)	Demo 4 (12%)	Demo 5 (9%)	Demo 6 (11%)
Flavor 1	72	67	40	22	36	30
Flavor 2	15	21	30	48	90	80
Flavor 3	40	61	79	67	42	50
Flavor 4	41	32	25	30	69	72

Demographic Groups. Low Price

Numbers represent consumer preference scores in market research (higher numbers mean better taste profile). Shading means that the flavor is in market. No color (i.e., white) means that the flavor is being tested for a potential launch. Circles represent which demographic group each flavor resonates most strongly with.

FIGURE 4.4 Hypothetical example of completed strategy map

listed by demographic group. The circles represent areas of strength based on the taste rating for each flavor. Under each demographic group is the percentage of the total volume of ketchup consumed. Based on the data shown here, which flavor would you recommend launching next, and why?

As another example, assume that you are the brand manager for Dell and are trying to help the sales department improve the number of Dell offerings at Best Buy. The Dell sales leader tells you that he believes that Best Buy doesn't have the right assortment of products. First, you decide to step back and try to understand where Best Buy is overdeveloped (i.e., has more than its typical share) and underdeveloped (i.e., has less than its typical share) relative to the general market. Once you understand how Best Buy is performing, you can then create a strategy map that the sales leader can use to help the Best Buy merchant understand how stocking specific Dell options can boost their PC business.

To accomplish this, you collect the following data: (1) key PC product segments, (2) general market share (across all consumer outlets) for each product segment, and (3) the retailer's sales across the various product segments. You then visualize overdevelopment (Best Buy has a higher percentage of business in a product segment relative to the general market) or underdevelopment (a lower percentage of business relative to the general market) by using the colors green (overdevelopment) and red (underdevelopment). This simple visualization will quickly communicate where Best Buy has strengths (overdevelopment) and opportunities (underdevelopment) and can be used to help the sales leader identify win-win opportunities—where Dell products can help improve the retailer's business.

In table 4.2, we can see in this fictitious example that Best Buy is underdeveloped in the "business performance" product segment across both low and high price points. They are also underdeveloped in the low-price "portability" segment. The sales leader could recommend stocking Dell's market-leading products in these segments to help the retailer address this unfulfilled consumer need.

TABLE 4.2

Example of a completed strategy map

Product Segment	Low Price	High Price	General Market Share[1]
Business Performance			25
Gaming Performance			20
Portability			15
Basic			40

[1]General Market Share: Total U.S. consumer market share across all outlets (excludes the direct-to-business market)
Light gray cells = Retailer's market share underdeveloped relative to the general market
Dark gray cells = Retailer's market share overdeveloped relative to the general market
Fictitious example created by author.

Time Required to Develop a Strategy Map

The time to develop a strategy map can vary significantly. In some cases, the data may be available, and you are simply trying to figure out how to consolidate it effectively for a specific audience. However, in other cases, you may not yet have the data. In these circumstances, you are essentially using the map framework as a guide to help direct your data acquisition and learning processes.

To illustrate how this can take a significant amount of time, let's look at an example from my past. I regularly used a variety of strategy maps to accomplish different goals. When I first landed in a global strategy department at one firm, the team needed to make sense of the global marketplace for a specific category of products. The objective was to understand how each individual brand was positioned relative to consumer needs to determine whether there was a "white space" opportunity (i.e., a consumer need on the map that no brand across the globe was yet delivering to). The central question was whether there was an opportunity to introduce a new brand or extend an existing brand as a mechanism for driving growth in these unaddressed areas of consumer need. In this case, the map took months to create because it was the final output of conducting global research into consumer needs, identifying the top brands and their positioning, and converting this information into a usable tool to aid in decision-making and communication. In this example, the map was a strategic tool designed first to help us understand the category, and then to communicate this insight and drive alignment.

Examples of the Types of Strategy Maps

Because there are a number of types of strategy maps, I will primarily discuss those that are more commonly used. Table 4.3 identifies five types of strategy maps and how they focus on internal capability development, consumer preferences, competitive dynamics, or a combination. In many cases, these popular examples are used to provide insight into more than one area (e.g., the BCG matrix provides insight into both internal resources and competitive positioning). While these are popular examples, strategy maps are simply tools that enable users to make better decisions and communicate more effectively. This means that an endless number of maps can be created depending on the purpose, data, and visualization chosen.

BCG Growth Share Matrix and McKinsey Matrix

Background: Created in the 1970s by Bruce Henderson, the founder of the Boston Consulting Group, the BCG growth share matrix[3] was designed to help companies prioritize businesses within a portfolio according to their competitiveness and the attractiveness of the market in which they compete.

Purpose: The purpose of the BCG growth share matrix is "a portfolio management framework that helps companies decide how

TABLE 4.3

Examples of popular strategy maps

	Internal Resources	Consumer Perceptions	Competitive Dynamics
BCG/McKinsey Matrix The BCC/McKinsey Matrix helps you manage your portfolio of businesses to drive growth on the firm level, by taking into account the market and competitive dynamics of each category.	✓		✓
Perceptual Map Perceptual maps provide a clean visual representation of what can be complicated consumer preference data, thus easily communicating how your products compare with competition in the same category.		✓	✓
Balanced Scorecard The balanced scorecard provides structure for internal discussion around business unit level key performance indicators that best ladder up to the company wide strategy and helps with the monitoring of efforts made to accomplish those goals.	✓		
Strategic Control The strategic control map provides a macro view of how your firm compares to competitors based on market capitalization.			✓
Payoff Matrix The payoff matrix helps you understand the potential financial impact of simple and simultaneous decisions between you and a competitor.			✓

to prioritize their different businesses by their degree of profitability."[4] It is a good tool for achieving internal alignment and clearly communicating the role of each line of business in a company portfolio.

In recent years, as the speed of change has accelerated, market share has become less of an indicator of advantage, but the matrix remains relevant because it can also be used to help manage investments toward strategic experimentation and innovation. The BCG matrix assumes that market share is an indicator of profitability and all growing markets are attractive. The McKinsey matrix (also known as the GE McKinsey matrix) is the same model, but it updates the axes to place industry attractiveness on one axis and business unit competitive advantage on the other.[5]

Components: To employ the BCG model, classify each product or business unit into one of the following four categories:

Dogs: In markets with low expected growth and little established share, it is usually recommended to divest or liquidate dogs, businesses or brands that show no potential.

Question marks: Lacking a clear direction forward, question marks are lines of business/brands that either should generally be divested or that require additional investment to become valuable.

Stars: With high market share and great opportunity for growth in their respective markets, star business units/brands are the best future performers in your portfolio.

Cash cows: As opposed to stars, the cash cows in your portfolio are typically steady cash flow generators, but in markets that are not growing. These businesses are often the heritage brands or businesses in a portfolio and are a great source of cash to invest in stars and question marks with potential.

Opportunities for use: The model is designed to help leaders think through various trade-off decisions, and either matrix is a good basis for discussion of the necessary prioritization that then follows.

Model in practice example: Figure 4.5 is an example of a matrix presenting various brands in the Unilever portfolio.

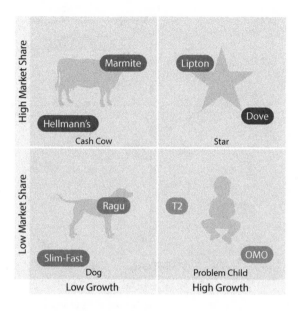

FIGURE 4.5 BCG strategy map for Unilever
Source: Tom Oakley (2014), "Unilever: BCG Matrix," *The Marketing Agenda*, available from: https://themarketingagenda.com/2014/09/20/unilever-bcg-matrix/

Perceptual Map

Purpose: With a simple visual layout, perceptual maps[6] easily convey how brands rank in terms of preference in the minds of consumers. Using *x*- and *y*-axes labeled with traits known to drive brand selection and differentiation, they present large amounts of complicated information in an easy-to-digest format. Whether you want to see where your brand currently fits in the market or to highlight where you want to shift a brand given the competitors, the perceptual map is an effective way to ensure that consumer preferences remain central to internal discussions and brand decisions.

Components: To get the maximum value out of a perceptual map, you must identify several pairs of traits that affect brand preference

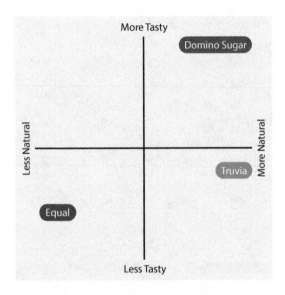

FIGURE 4.6 Perceptual map for the sugar and sugar-substitute markets
Source: Ben Cohen (2016), "What Perceptual Brand Mapping Can Do for You and Your Business," Denneen & Company, available from: http://denneen.com/what -perceptual-brand-mapping-can-do-for-you-and-your-business/

and create multiple maps. Having more than one map forces you to see the same market from different perspectives.

Opportunities for use: In a world where Big Data is increasingly easy to collect and access, this model is a great way to convey a lot of complicated information about consumer preferences within your brand's category in a very simple format.

Model in practice example 1: Figure 4.6 shows a map for the sugar and sugar-substitute markets, looking at the degree to which the products are perceived to be natural and tasty.

Model in practice example 2: The perceptual map in figure 4.7 was used to demonstrate why the classic retailer, Gap, has been struggling in recent years. The point it makes is that the brand didn't have a strong image among consumers on the "fashion/value equation."

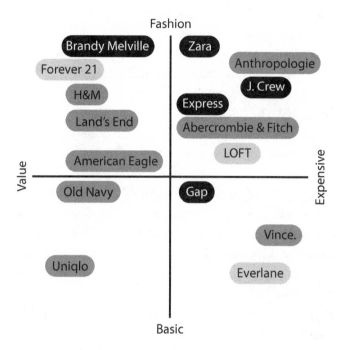

FIGURE 4.7 Perceptual map for retailers
Source: Ashley Lutz (2014), "This Chart Shows Gap's Biggest Problem," *Business Insider*, available from: http://www.businessinsider.com/gap-shopping-brand-chart-2014-5

Balanced Scorecard

Background: Originally created by Dr. Robert Kaplan and Dr. David Norton, the balanced scorecard (BSC)[7] was designed to help organizations create a *balanced* set of key performance indicators to help shift company focus from short-term to long-term success. The BSC is a type of strategy map that is popular across a number of types of companies and industries because of its strength in combining both big-picture strategy elements and more tactical activities.

Purpose: BSC maps are used to visually communicate how value in an organization is created by tracking one key performance indicator for each perspective of the larger strategy. The BSC is used by organizations to accomplish four key tasks: (1) communicate the strategic vision; (2) align the day-to-day work with the higher-level strategy; (3) prioritize specific projects, products, and services; and (4) evaluate progress toward strategic goals.

Components: The BSC map recommends viewing an organization from the following four perspectives and then developing and organizing targets and actions under each perspective:

Financial (referred to as "Stewardship" in the public sector): Review a firm's performance through a financial lens and evaluate the allocation and use of financial resources.

Customer/stakeholder: Review the performance of the firm through the lens of customer and other stakeholder satisfaction and/or retention.

Internal process: Review the performance of the firm from the perspective of the quality and efficiency of the products and services.

Organizational capacity: Review the firm's performance through the lens of technology, culture, human capital, and infrastructure.

Opportunities for use: The BSC map is useful for obtaining an internal review of how an organization is tracking against multiple key performance indicators specific to each strategic element.

Model in practice example: Table 4.4 gives a visual of the key strategic priorities for a hypothetical accounting firm across the four perspectives summarized here.

Strategic Control

Background: The strategic control map[8] was developed in 1996 by McKinsey's Vijay D'Silva, Bob Fallon, and Asheet Mehta as a way for companies to use market capitalization to identify potential

TABLE 4.4

Balanced scorecard for hypothetical accounting firm

	Strategy Objectives	Measures	Targets	Initiatives
Financial	Increase market share and profit margin	• Market share	• Market share > 5%	• Increase targeted marketing efforts
		• Profit margin	• Profit margin increase of 10%	• Reduce overhead by eliminating office space
Customer	Improve customer satisfaction and retention	• Customer satisfaction	• Net promoter score >75	• Customer satisfaction survey and follow-up
		• Customer lifetime value	• CLU increase +10%	
Internal business processes	Track customer feedback throughout process	• Measure customer feedback at eight points of engagement	• Measurement system in place within 12 months	• Customer feedback system
Learning and growth	Monitor customer feedback and train the organization on improving client engagement	• Number of training sessions • Organization's feedback on tracking efficacy	• 100 training sessions in fiscal year	• Customer engagement training

companies that could be strong acquisition targets. Understanding this view provides a clear picture of the performance of a firm relative to its competition by evaluating the relationship between a firm's size (measured in book value) and its performance (measured by market-to-book ratio).

Purpose: The objective of this map is to identify acquisition targets and to identify and avoid potential takeover threats. The placement within one of the four quadrants of the strategic control map helps indicate the strategic challenges and opportunities that a company uniquely faces relative to its competition.

Components: The axes focus on communicating performance and relative size, as follows:

> In the upper-right quadrant are large, high-performing compa-
> nies that are the least likely to be acquisition targets. Instead,
> they face the challenge of maintaining their strong position
> by continuing to find and foster new opportunities without
> limiting their expected returns.
>
> In contrast, companies in the lower-left quadrant are likely tar-
> gets for potential divestiture, as they have poorer performance
> and are smaller in size.
>
> Companies in the upper-left quadrant tend to have intellectual
> property assets or portfolios that provide financial returns, as
> well as a competitive advantage through propriety knowledge.
>
> The large companies in the bottom-right quadrant need to find
> ways to improve their performance, or else they probably will
> become targets for buyers looking to achieve value through
> efficiencies enabled by cost-cutting and consolidation.

Opportunities for use: The strategic control map helps a company understand what balance of size and performance will enable it to continue to grow successfully and avoid takeover. To see an example in practice, look at an article published by *McKinsey Quarterly* for a strategic control map for thirty countries.[9]

Payoff Matrix

Background: The payoff matrix[10] highlights the potential payoff for a strategic decision made by one company in the context of anticipated countermoves by competitors. Usually presented as a 2×2 matrix with two players and two decisions, larger matrices can be used for more complex scenarios. Payoff matrices work best when there are a discreet number of players and decisions related to pricing, product design, research and development, promotion, and other elements.

Purpose: The payoff matrix helps identify strategies that will give your company a competitive advantage.

Components: To create a payoff matrix, begin by identifying the competitors and decisions or moves that you would like to analyze. Next, compile data on the payoff for each decision for each player, using tools such as discounted cash flows and sensitivity analysis. Given that payoff matrices assume a single round of simultaneous decisions, once you understand and lay out the potential payoffs, you can identify the dominant strategy for your firm regardless of the competitive responses to your decisions.

Opportunities for use: Payoff matrices help predict potential reactions among competitors and provide a simple visualization for leaders of potential financial outcomes as a consequence of making different decisions.

Model in practice example: The fictional example shown in figure 4.8 shows a potential payoff for Tide versus Purex laundry detergent if they simultaneously made moves to increase or lower their prices. Tide's payouts are indicated in bold to help visually differentiate the expected results.

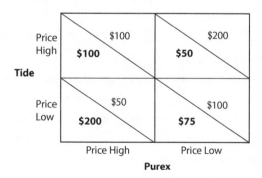

FIGURE 4.8 Payoff matrix for Tide versus Purex

Summary

This chapter has introduced the concept of strategy maps, tools that can help marketers better understand complex information, make better decisions, align key organizational stakeholders, and sell a point of view to clients or customers. There is no shortage of articles and books that talk about the power of storytelling to sell. A key way in which marketing strategists tell stories is through strategy maps, as these visually summarize a story through the language of business.

To conclude, I share with you one last story about the power of strategy maps. When I worked as the CMO of a fashion retailer, I arrived at the company at a time in which some businesses were aggressively shifting from traditional media channels to digital. As I assessed our marketing investment relative to the usefulness of each channel for the target (i.e., importance in driving decisions) and the value to the business (i.e., ability to drive sales), our allocation was heavily invested in low-usefulness/low-value activities. In other words, we were investing a lot of money in channels that neither were useful to the consumer nor led to sales. However, the company had always anchored investment behavior on a "comp" mentality. In retail, comp store sales are a key measure that tracks performance versus the same period a year ago. With this mindset, we were stuck in a pattern of essentially spending on the same activities at the same levels year after year, despite the fact that the market and the consumers had shifted.

I knew that by shifting resources, we could deliver growth more effectively at a lower investment level—something that profit-and-loss (P&L) marketing leaders are taught to do. The challenge in front of me was figuring out how to convince the CEO and board, who had a comp mindset, to be willing to break out of the norm and test moving toward a more efficient and effective approach. The key for me to sell my vision was to create a convincing image. I knew that I wanted to share a visual—it would be more effective than writing the recommendation. I then created an image that included the following information in one picture: return on investment (ROI), consumer usage, investment allocation, and projected key competitor allocation by media type.

A key reason that companies hire consultants is to convert complex information into stories about how the business works and what should be done to address a key problem. To tell these stories, consultants use presentations comprised of strategy map after strategy map. As business leaders, we are not born with this skill; rather, we must develop, refine, and hone the ability to use strategy maps effectively. It simply takes awareness of what strategy maps are and practice at using them to become expert. In chapter 10 of this book, I will share ways in which you can gain proficiency in their use.

BRIDGING TOOLS—FROM
STRATEGY TO IMPLEMENTATION

5

The Strategic Marketing Plan

(Strategy). It's about winning. It's not about just playing the game. It's about winning, and you need to be very clear what winning means. In our view, it means three things—uniquely positioning a firm in its industry, creating sustainable advantage and delivering superior value versus the competition. It's important that you make the necessary choices to get all three elements right. . . . There's a mindset among CEOs and other leaders that they don't want to get pinned down or painted into a corner. They want to keep all their options open. Why do they want that? Because they don't want to take on the risk of making a bad choice or a wrong choice. But the fact is, strategy is all about making choices—choosing where you're going to play and how you're going to win, along with what winning means.

—A. G. LAFLEY, CEO OF PROCTER AND GAMBLE[1]

THUS FAR, THE CHAPTERS in this book have focused on strategy-setting tools such as the positioning concept, the brand essence statement (BES), and strategy maps. These tools help create a vision of where the brand or business should play in order to drive growth. However, converting a marketing strategy into plans that can achieve a vision is often more difficult than devising an effective strategy in the first place. Yet look at most textbooks, managerial books, and executive education courses. How many focus on strategy? How many, in contrast, focus on effective implementation? How many of us would rather take a course entitled "Developing Successful Strategies," as opposed to a course entitled "Successful Implementation"?

If we're being honest, most of us would rather invest our time thinking about, and learning about, strategy. However, great marketing strategy is successful only if the firm implements it effectively.

The next two chapters, therefore, introduce bridging tools—methods that enable marketing strategists to effectively convert strategy into plans. In this chapter, the focus is on understanding how to define strategies and plans that will enable the marketing strategist to lead the firm to achieve positional advantage.

What Is a Strategic Marketing Plan?

First, let's take a step back and think about how much we really know about strategy. "Strategy" is a term thrown around in meeting after meeting, boardroom after boardroom—it's not rare to hear, "The strategy is . . ." It is as if just saying the words ensures that there *is* a strategy and that it will enable a brand to create a sustainable competitive advantage. And yet, from organizations to CEOs to even government officials, there is a failure to have clear, coherent, and winnable strategies. It is rumored that on the day of Kmart's bankruptcy, there were 100 priorities on the CEO's whiteboard. As you'll see throughout the rest of this chapter, having 100 priorities is an indication of a company that has failed to identify the few strategic choices needed to win. So, what is strategy?

> Strategy is the pattern of decisions that determines and reveals its objectives, purposes, or goals, produces the principal policies and plans for achieving those goals, and defines the range of business the company is to pursue, the kind of economic and human organization it is or intends to be, and the nature of the economic and noneconomic contribution it intends to make to its shareholders, employees, customers, and communities.[2]

A strategic plan, then, is a set of limited choices that direct and focus activity to achieve an overall goal.

Consequently, a strategic *marketing* plan defines the set of choices regarding how the business/brand will create positional advantage that delivers profitable growth. The choice set is anchored on creating better solutions (relative to competitors) that address consumer problems, needs, and desires. There are three important principles associated with a strategic marketing plan. First, strategy requires that you decide what to do—and what *not to do*. One of the most difficult challenges is to identify the fewest number of strategies that will ensure you achieve your goals. To do this, you must make trade-offs that identify what you have chosen *not* to do.[3] Second, the specific strategies that the marketer chooses must have a complementary interaction. In other words, each individual brand strategy must fit well with the other strategies created. Finally, the strategic marketing plan must work with the strategic plans created by other functions and/or business units. As such, strategic plans work in a cascading manner: The CEO's strategic plan sets the boundary and priorities for the firm. Strategic plans set forth by other top management leaders (CMO, CFO, CHRO, CIO) work in synch with one another to deliver the CEO's strategic plan, and this continues throughout each level of the organization.[4] As a result, the strategic marketing plan sits at the intersection of the firm's strategic plan and marketing operations, serving as a road map for defining the few critical, marketing-related choices that must be executed flawlessly to help marketing—and the firm—achieve positional advantage and growth.

As the output (typically a document) of a structured process, the strategic marketing plan serves three purposes: (1) it serves as a road map to guide departmental actions; (2) it is a useful tool for communicating marketing plans with channel partners, board members, strategic partners, peers, and other stakeholders; and (3) it serves as a loose form of contract against which the CEO can hold the CMO accountable. If you work in a marketing department, regardless of level (whether a brand assistant or EVP of marketing) a strategic marketing plan helps align your work with that of the department, align key stakeholders, and serve as an annual contract with your boss and organization.

So why do marketers and other leaders struggle to develop effective strategic plans? The reality is that it is significantly more difficult than most people think to create an *effective* strategic plan. Whether it is developing a superior positioning concept, BES, or strategic marketing plan, all these activities require practice, experience, and time to become proficient. The tendency is to think that just because a plan is created, it is a strong plan. And this isn't the case. While two leaders can both create strategic marketing plans, one likely has a better chance of success than the other given market conditions, firm capabilities, and resources. A superior strategic plan enables leaders to articulate a vision and ensure that the entire organization is working in alignment with the few strategies chosen in order to build a superior brand or business.

Although the strategic planning process takes time and resources to develop, it is an important period during the hustle and bustle of executing programs in which to step back, evaluate the broad landscape, assess the state of the current business, and determine where the firm is headed and how marketing can play a role in achieving firm-level goals. Just as somebody taking a vacation doesn't just start driving without planning the route beforehand, it's important for marketers, especially in leadership positions, to take time to reflect on progress and make sure that the path the organization is headed down makes sense given the current circumstances.

Who Creates a Strategic Marketing Plan?

Typically, the individual who manages the marketing function will be responsible for creating a departmental strategic plan, but this may vary across firms. For example, some companies are organized by product or geography, not by function. In these circumstances, the divisional, brand, or product leader is likely to create a strategic plan, a component of which may be related to marketing. Regardless of who creates the strategic marketing plan at the firm, the process typically flows from the corporate plan to ensure that all departments are aligned with the firm's overall strategic plan.

The Process of Developing a Strategic Marketing Plan

Generally, there is a significant amount of background work that goes into creating and evaluating strategic options and determining the optimal path for marketing to take, given the set of circumstances facing the firm. These inputs include an understanding of the external marketplace, including the competition and consumers. This insight is then combined with an understanding of internal factors, including the firm's annual strategic plan, capabilities including marketing and other functions such as research and development (R&D), and marketing resources, to develop a strategic marketing plan.

In an organization with a well-defined strategic planning process, similar types of input are used by each top management team (TMT) leader (e.g., the CMO, CIO/CTO, CFO, general counsel CAO, and CHRO) to come up with strategic plans at the departmental level.[5] Once these are aligned across the TMT and the CEO, the strategic planning process continues to cascade down through all levels (figure 5.1). Using this cascading process ensures that each individual within the firm has a strategic plan linked to their functional plan, which then synchronizes with the corporate plan.

The amount of time it takes to go through this process can vary. Some companies have an elaborate, data-based approach that can take up to six months to complete. Others may have a less sophisticated process that takes only a few days. Unfortunately, there are a number of firms, even large, respected ones, that don't have a firmwide strategic planning process. The lack of a strategic planning process can make a firm vulnerable to competitors for several reasons: (1) the TMT isn't aligned on strategic priorities, (2) individual departments may operate at cross-purposes because they aren't tethered together by any central strategic plan, and (3) the firm wastes resources (both money and labor) as individual TMT leaders work on departmental priorities rather than priorities that flow from the overall firm objectives. Imagine a baseball team where each individual position has no

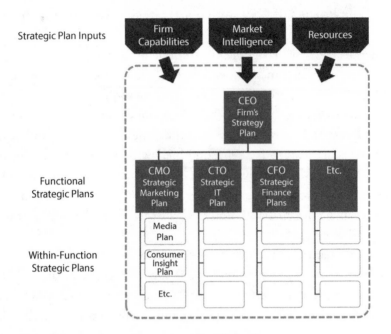

Strategic Plan Inputs

Functional
Strategic Plans

Within-Function
Strategic Plans

FIGURE 5.1 The cascading effect of strategic planning

clear guidelines that support the team's overall strategy. Without strategic alignment across and within departments, a disjointed organization may only be the beginning of the firm's challenges. As Yogi Berra suggested, "If you don't know where you are going, you'll end up someplace else."[6]

The Five Parts of a Strategic Marketing Plan

There are nearly as many different strategic marketing plan formats as there are firms, so there is no one right format. The specific format is less important than the process that the firm goes through to identify the strategic plan and align departments and individuals throughout the organization. While there are a number of strategic planning formats used, the following sections are common to many of them (see the chapter appendix for samples).

1. **Vision**: An important aspect of leadership is the ability to articulate an aspirational position (i.e., vision) regarding where the business will be at some point in the future. As a key part of the strategic marketing plan, the vision is a set of words used to describe a future state (e.g., three or five years in the future) and is the one area of the strategic marketing plan that is longer-term in nature. It sets a stake in the ground to show where the brand (or business) should be in the future and helps to focus the organization on an end point that is more than twelve months away.

2. **Objectives**: Objectives define, in numerical terms, the results that the strategic marketing plan is designed to achieve *within* the next twelve months (or some shorter-term period of time that suits the firm or department). Ideally, these objectives should align, in some way, with firm-level objectives. For example, if the firm wants to achieve revenue and profit growth of 5 percent, marketing could have the primary responsibility for achieving the revenue growth part of the goal. As such, this section of the strategic marketing plan would include both the growth percentage and the specific number of cases associated with that growth (e.g., "5 percent revenue growth compared to the previous year; 10 million cases"). It's important to be precise so you can easily measure the results at the end of the year. Any ambiguity will make it difficult to track and measure performance.

   The strategic plan may include a combination of financial objectives and market-based objectives (e.g., customer satisfaction, market share). For example, marketing could be charged with "increasing customer satisfaction from 90 percent to 91 percent." Regardless of the objectives chosen, there are four criteria that the "Objectives" section must meet: it must (1) be synchronized with firm-level objectives, (2) be specific and measurable, (3) ensure that marketing has the authority and ability to largely determine the outcome of the measures, and (4) limit the number of objectives to as few as possible (ideally, just one) to help focus departmental efforts.

3. **Strategies**: Arguably one of the most difficult parts of the strategic marketing plan to write, the "Strategies" section identifies the smallest number of strategies that are most likely to ensure that marketing accomplishes the chosen objectives. Typically, the organization will focus on no more than five strategies that—if executed well—will increase their odds of success.

   Developing the three to five strategies that in combination will yield the greatest chance of brand/business success is a difficult task. Consider a circle. Within that circle are 100 possible ideas to accomplish your business objectives (similar to the 100 priorities on the Kmart CEO's whiteboard). You notice that when you look at all the activities, they fall into roughly fifteen buckets (let's consider these buckets to be fifteen strategic areas for the purpose of illustrating this point). For example, you have one strategic area that has a set of activities related to strengthening the brand, another that is related to the training and development of the department, another related to innovation, and so on. You realize that you cannot effectively undertake all 100 activities. Further, you realize that tackling only one or two activities in each of the fifteen strategic areas means that you will poorly execute all the possible strategies. You conclude that you must pick the three to five strategic areas of activities that will yield the greatest chance of success. Which areas do you choose? Which do you easily eliminate, and which are you concerned about eliminating? How do you choose?

This method is a tactics-to-strategy approach of defining your strategies. For individuals who are just beginning to develop strategic plans, it can be a useful approach to understanding the difference between strategies and tactics. With practice, you will be able to identify strategic areas directly from the objectives.

This section of the strategic planning process is crucial for establishing the greatest chance of success. In the 2012 presidential election, Mitt Romney was derided for having a fifty-nine-point economic plan.[7] The argument was that voters were confused over what Romney wanted to do because they couldn't comprehend a fifty-nine-point plan for turning the economy around; furthermore, the laundry list of activities signaled that Romney was more of an operator than a strategic leader. Juxtapose this lack of strategic clarity with fellow presidential candidate Herman Cain's "9-9-9 Plan" (a plan to replace the complex tax system with a 9 percent personal income tax, 9 percent sales tax, and 9 percent corporate tax). It was simple and memorable, and it signaled a degree of strategic focus. Which do you think might be more likely to ensure that an organization (in this case the federal government) is aligned in their execution? When leading an organization, whether it is a country or a company, everybody following you must be able to comprehend and follow your strategic choices.

As an example of a simple-to-understand strategic priority list, consider PetSmart's strategic priorities during its turnaround, when the company migrated from PetsMart (a warehouse shopping experience) to PetSmart (a retail experience targeting high-end, pet-involved consumers). It's possible to condense the company's strategic priorities, outlined in its annual reports, into three distinct areas: (1) Delight the customer, (2) Operational excellence, and (3) Grow services.

The firm's priority projects fit within this simple framework and could be used to direct employees' efforts, whether they stocked shelves, managed a store, or worked in marketing. New employees could be trained to understand and remember the strategic plan, (using an acronym of "DOG") and to see how their actions help deliver on the strategic choices. This is an example of how a smart—and well-thought-out—strategic plan can direct an army of employees deployed across a continent such that they act in unison and with purpose.

Interestingly, while business schools often prioritize quantitative and analytical skills, there isn't an algorithm that can determine which three to five strategic priorities (of the fifteen mentioned in the previous example) are the optimal ones to choose. Identifying the best set of strategies takes a lot of practice. This is why those who are in a position to determine the direction of an organization (or firm) often shoulder greater responsibility and, as a consequence, accountability when plans fail to achieve their objectives. There is almost no way to know for sure which strategic priorities will generate the best results. Thus, companies put faith in individuals who have proved that they can create and execute superior strategies that have led to successful results in the past. This is often why strategic planning—and implementation—skills are more important in ascending to the C-suite than many other skills.

As you develop strategies (such as those described in the appendix), it's important to write them clearly while allowing latitude for the tactics that you will choose within each strategic area. The strategies should ideally be more general, allowing for leeway in how to implement the strategies; as a result, the strategies could focus on a marketing activity area, such as analytics, innovation, branding, organizational design, training, or strategic partnerships, or a business area such as e-commerce, business-to-business (B2B) revenue generation, catalog sales, or store sales.

The following story was shared with me during a conversation with the head of marketing for a leading retailer. The CMO inherited a department that didn't have agreed-to key performance indicators, dashboards, sophisticated analyses, reporting tools, or deep consumer understanding. For the department to increase marketing return on investment (MROI), the CMO believed that they needed to invest in tools, systems, and processes to improve their analytical and reporting capabilities. Therefore, the created strategy focused on "improving departmental performance via more consumer-centric insight, data-based analysis, and disciplined processes that informed program development, tracked progress, and measured performance." This is much broader than a tactic, such as "create a dashboard," which in fact was one of the tactics required to deliver this strategy.

But while the strategy shouldn't be too specific (i.e., tactical), it also can't be too general (e.g., "fix analytical systems"), as it doesn't provide enough direction. Essentially, strategies are a middle ground between broad and narrow.

Hint: For those who have never developed strategies before, a good way to practice is to walk through the circle exercise previously mentioned. One way I practiced early in my career was use to strategic planning for personal goals. Suppose that you want to develop a strategic plan to save $10,000 (or any specific amount of money that makes sense for you) within five years. A way to identify the optimal three to five strategies is to start by listing every activity that you can do to save the money. You then group these activities into similar buckets. For example, one bucket might center on cutting expenses, and another might center on becoming more educated about financial investment. When you are done with this exercise, try to identify the three to five buckets that you think are most important in helping you accomplish your objective. Then evaluate whether these three to five areas are the most effective when used in combination. Over time, and with practice, you will be able to create strategic options without having to use bucket tactics to do so.

4. **Tactics:** Once you have identified your strategic priorities, the next step is to determine the optimal set of tactics within each strategic bucket that you want to execute. An important consideration at this point is the resources that you have at your disposal; developing too many tactics at once can lead to failure if you have neither the staff (i.e., capability or time) nor the budget. The ultimate goal is to identify the smallest number of tactics that will enable you to deliver the strategy, while also ensuring that the tactics are as granular and specific as possible. As in the process of identifying strategies, you want to look at the set of tactics as a group to ensure that they complement one another, thus creating a synergistic effect. Following through with the retail example from before, the CMO chose as one of the tactics: "Develop a brand image dashboard that measures functional and emotional attributes versus importance and versus competition monthly (due date: June)." You also want to include a target date for completion. By doing this, the strategist is able to connect the dots from corporate strategy to marketing strategy to tactics to a delivery date— all on just one page.

5. **Measures:** Deciding which measures to capture on the strategic marketing plan is crucial. The measures identify specifically how you will measure your progress and success against each of the three to five strategies that you have chosen. If you have one strategy that is anchored on strengthening the brand, how will you know whether you have succeeded? Revenue performance? Margin improvement? Customer experience measures? Brand image measures?

Concept testing measures? Social media valence measures? Loyalty measures? These critical decisions will help serve as a filter through which to assess the specific tactics you've selected. If you've chosen strengthening the brand as your primary strategy and your measure is "brand image rating on quality," tactics centered on improving the customer's service experience likely won't improve performance on that measure. The strategies, tactics, and measures must all align.

Key Principles in Developing a Strong Strategic Plan

While there is variance across marketing plan formats, content, and processes, there are some essential principles to keep in mind.

1. **It should be a stand-alone document.** The marketing plan should be excellently written, with deliberate word choices. It should not require an interpreter, a translator, or additional documents in order to understand it.

2. **It should reflect ruthless choice-making.** The enemy of excellence is trying to do everything. Superior results require superior choice-making regarding what you will and won't do. In general, this is a challenge for many people. The educational system largely teaches you to do everything on your "homework" list. There isn't a lot of opportunity to consciously pick and choose priorities. Practicing this skill, even in your personal life (i.e., setting health goals, personal goals, or financial goals), can enhance your ability to become an effective strategist.

3. **It cannot be created in isolation.** Great strategic plans require "workshopping," where you share them with key partners, employees, and mentors to collect perspective, insight, and feedback. While you are the decision-maker, the more insight

you get from those with whom you work, trust, and respect, the stronger a plan will be—and the easier it will be to sell it to other stakeholders.

4. **It should align with the annual goals against which the department will be reviewed.** The way in which the department and the CMO are measured should align with the strategic plan. For example, if the CMO is measured on return on invested capital (ROIC) but the strategies are centered on building an analytics-oriented organization, strengthening the brand, and developing an external strategic partnership program, how will accomplishing these strategies deliver ROIC? If they aren't synchronized, you may want to recommend to your boss that you add a couple of measures to your annual review (or consider shifting your strategic plan).

5. **Remember that strategic plans often require a sequencing of strategies.** For example, a CMO of a luxury brand took over a marketing department that was relying on old technology and had a dearth of consumer data and insight. The company's same-store comp sales were declining, so there was an urgent need to turn around the business. After a thorough investigation, the CMO realized that the technology infrastructure and the human resource infrastructure (marketing talent, training, and organizational structure) were subpar. The CMO created a vision to be the preeminent firm in the category, but year one was centered on a five-pronged strategy to first build the infrastructure: (1) systems, (2) processes, (3) structure, (4) reporting, and (5) people. While there was pressure to add programs, innovate, and invest in strengthening the brand, the CMO used the strategic planning process and document to help the board, peers, and CEO understand that without the right infrastructure, investment in innovation or brand would be wasted. For example, the group didn't have a dashboard that enabled upper management to

understand the efficacy of email campaigns. Investing more money in campaigns without any mechanism to assess ROI was fruitless.

Testing Whether You Have a Strong Strategic Marketing Plan

Once you have drafted the strategic marketing plan, you should step back and make sure that it has internal consistency, meaning that all elements of the plan work together in unity, and ideally synergistically. To help assess whether your strategic marketing plan does this, you should be able to answer "yes" to the following questions:

1. **Will the three to five strategies chosen, if executed excellently, have a high probability of meeting the objectives?** If not, go back and reevaluate your strategic choices.
2. **Are you sure that the next two strategies (on your list) not chosen are the correct ones to eliminate from your strategic priorities?** You are essentially looking at where you drew the line regarding your strategies and making sure that you are confident that the ones that you included are appropriate and the ones that you excluded were indeed the ones to eliminate.
3. **Are the tactics chosen the best fit for the strategies being pursued?** You are looking for a fit between each individual strategy and the group of tactics chosen.
4. **If you deliver all these measures successfully, will you have a high chance of achieving your overall objective?** This is a test to ensure that the activities you are focused on and the measures of your performance against these activities will enable you to meet your objective.
5. **If the strategies, tactics, and measures are all delivered excellently, will you make progress toward the vision that you have created?** If not, then you have created a strategic marketing

plan that is disconnected from your vision. The actions that you take this year should help move the brand toward the vision you created.

Summary

Developing a skill in strategic thinking is a valuable capability, especially in mid- to senior-level positions. And yet it takes practice. The more you write strategic plans, the more adept you become at thinking strategically. You naturally start prioritizing activities and critically assessing the strategic decisions being made around you. When political candidates talk about their strategies for fixing the economy, you have a better ability to critically analyze their priorities. When the head of the Parent Teacher Association presents a strategic plan for enhancing the group's performance, you can evaluate the plan for internal consistency and the likelihood that the choices made will achieve the objectives. In summary, there is an art and a science to developing strategic marketing plans, and practice—accompanied by feedback and living with the consequences of your choices—is the best way to gain skill.

Appendix

Vision:

Objective	Strategies	Measures	Tactics

FIGURE AP 5.1 Format example 1: Strategic plan, horizontal format

Long-Term Vision:

Fiscal Year Objective:

Strategy 1:	Strategy 1:	Strategy 1:
Measures:	Measures:	Measures:
Tactics:	Tactics:	Tactics:

FIGURE AP 5.2 Format example 2: Strategic plan, vertical format

P&G Alumni Network Strategic Plan Short Form

This provides the updated Action Plan for 2014/15 – 2019/20.

Mission – We are a group of business professionals with the shared experience of having worked for Procter & Gamble. We have come together to serve our alumni around the world both personally and professionally and give back to society.

Vision – Our vision is to harness the skills and talents of this remarkable group of people for both their personal growth and to the benefit of the communities in which we live and work and to become the most respected and most highly regarded business alumni organization in the world

Purpose/Goals – The Network exists with two primary purposes in mind:

- Facilitating the connections between and among alumni for either professional/ business reasons or solely personal reasons.
- Giving back to the communities and organizations in which our members are meaningfully involved.

The Network is intended to be a confederation of independent chapters rather than a centralized association that defines the activities of the individual chapters.

Who We Serve – The Network is a global organization serving:

- Our Members – The underlying intention is to build an organization of individuals with shared experiences that are the result of being employed by P&G. We do not differentiate between individuals who retired from the Company or those who left to join another organization.

- Our Chapters – Our primary vehicle for serving the membership on a regular basis is the confederation of chapters around the world. We anticipate that the needs of the chapter network will be different from the needs of the individual members themselves and we believe that to serve the members, we will need to understand the particular needs of the chapters.

- Our Philanthropic Beneficiaries – Our philanthropy is driven by the interests of our members and chapters. We have defined philanthropy as contributing our expertise, time, and financial resources to activities which focus on economic empowerment through business education, entrepreneurship, economic development and inclusion, and free enterprise.

How We Serve/Action Plans – The attached chart shows the specific activities we intend to use to serve our audiences, meet our goals, and achieve our vision. This document provides our proposed plans for the next five year period. Importantly, the action plans have been broken down and sequenced in recognition of our limited resources as a volunteer organization.

Serving Members – We will serve individual P&G alumni by connecting them to and with other alumni. In this context we will focus on:

1. Membership – Membership has now reached 35,000. And continues to grow. To drive growth even further, we will increase our focus in this area with the ultimate objective of engaging all Procter & Gamble alumni globally. A newly formed Membership Committee will help with both understanding the wants/needs of the members and executing membership building programs. We will conduct research to help us identify the latest services and values the Network can and

* Procter & Gamble and P&G are trade names of The Procter & Gamble Company and are used pursuant to an agreement with The Procter & Gamble Company. P&G Alumni Network is an independent organization apart from The Procter & Gamble Company.

FIGURE AP 5.3 Strategic marketing plan example 1: P&G Alumni network

should provide to the members. Additionally, we will ensure that the Membership Committee head is a regular contributor to the Board meetings, with metrics established and tracked.

2. Communications -- We have strong communication tools in place (web site, LinkedIn, email blast capabilities, etc). We will continue to review the latest available applications in all areas, and specifically designed for alumni websites to continue to drive alumni utilization of the various tools, keeping in mind the financial requirements of such improvements. We propose to include regular tracking of metrics in the monthly Board reports.

3. Global Conferences – We continue to deliver excellent programs and get solid satisfaction scores from the members who attend our bi-annual conferences. Both the Toronto and Geneva events were able to deliver revenues in excess of expenses to allow for the operation of the Network and the Foundation. We will continue to field a Global Conference every other year with the location shifting between major geographies. It is essential that we maintain the value of these events lest we "wear out" the membership and our sponsors. This is a function of both maintaining/increasing the value of the event and holding down the cost to the members who attend.

4. Women's Forum – The Women's Forum continues to provide an important contribution to the bi-annual global conferences. We wish to ensure that the opportunities for women to share and learn from each other go beyond the general conference. We will establish two subcommittees of the Women's Forum. The first will continue to focus on involvement with the global conferences, while the second will be charged with integrating the Women's Forum at the chapter level. The both of these committees will be invited to regularly attend and present on the Board of Director calls.

Serving Chapters – We have nearly 50 chapters across 37+ countries at varying degrees of development. We will help existing chapters thrive and help new chapters get established. In this context we will focus on:

1. Existing Chapters – We will increase our focus on (i) re-energizing chapters that have not yet taken root; (ii) supporting our healthiest chapters to maximize their value to the membership; and (iii) integrate the women's forum learning (and other learning related to women leaders) into the chapters. We will create a regional framework to allow the chapters to more easily share best practices. Further, we are undertaking additional research to better understand the new and existing services that the global network can/should provide for both the members and the chapters. We plan to include the Chairperson of the Chapter/Membership committee as a regular ad hoc member on the Board calls in order to maintain the focus of the organization on this key area. We will also establish a more formal communications effort, e.g. regular e-publications, to keep the membership regularly informed of:

   - the services available from the Network
   - events scheduled across the chapters and at the Network level
   - jobs and other opportunities
   - charitable giving
   - sponsor messages

   While each of these is currently available on the web site, we will encourage greater and more regular outbound communications.

2. New Chapters – We will focus on adding new, healthy chapters in major markets e.g., in the Middle East and India, History suggests that the key to success is to identify strong, committed leadership at the regional and chapter level in order to accomplish these objectives. We will link the emerging new chapters with existing chapters, share with the new chapters our best practices including possible legal/tax/insurance needs, and share content/speaker

Procter & Gamble and P&G are trade names of The Procter & Gamble Company and are used pursuant to an agreement with The Procter & Gamble Company. P&G Alumni Network is an independent organization apart from The Procter & Gamble Company.

resources/sponsorship learning and more.

<u>Serving Philanthropic Beneficiaries in Which are Members are Meaningfully Involved</u> – We will continue to help drive our three-tiers of philanthropy – (i) as a Global Network; (ii) through our chapters, and (iii) through individual members. This serves our goal to give back to society while making our members proud to be part of the Network. In this context we will focus on:

1. <u>Global Philanthropic Giving</u> – With nearly a decade of grant giving, we have been able to continue to improve the grant making process and have maintained a strong number of requests from around the world as we increase our ability to deliver funds. With the recent establishment of our 501(c)3 P&G Alumni Foundation, the grant making portion of our mission has shifted to the Foundation while the Network continues to serve as the fundraising arm of the group.
2. <u>Global Philanthropic Revenue Generation</u> -- In addition to monetary support of philanthropies, the organization has developed vehicles to harness the expertise of our members (published our first book, started our speaker's bureau, and developed webinars/seminars) which will help: (i) generate revenues from these programs which would be funneled back into our philanthropic efforts; and (ii) provide a benefit for others (including members and non members, businesses, schools, non-profits, NGOs, governments, etc.) With the speaker's bureau and webinars demonstrating stronger financial potential than publishing, we will focus marketing efforts in these two areas. We will expand the committee to provide increased support for the speaker's bureau and webinars/seminars. Additionally, we have started work on development of a $25MM endowment. We are evaluating the opportunity to hire an Executive Director to lead the fundraising effort. We will review the Endowment campaign as we progress to determine if we need to make adjustments.
3. <u>Chapter Philanthropy</u> – Many chapters have developed strong philanthropy programs at the chapter level. We will share their learnings across the Network and help them leverage the Network website to facilitate their efforts.
4. <u>Individual Philanthropy</u> – We will continue to offer the opportunity for individual members to share their needs/results with the network via the Members Helping Members section of our web site.

<u>Building the Network Brand</u> – We will continue to put the tools in place to execute publications, speaking engagements, webinars, etc. which are consistent with the Network brand promise we are trying to create. As we move more aggressively in the execution of our programs, we will remain cognizant of the brand and the promise we intend to build.

<u>Driving Multi-Stream Funding</u> – We continue to appreciate the funding from P&G as well as bi-annual sponsorship support from Publicis Groupe, Omnicom, and WPP. As we look to expand our network, invest in new communication and marketing tools, and drive funding for the P&G Alumni Foundation grants, we will seek opportunities to: (a) generate revenue from additional sources; and (b) maintain strict control of our expenses.

* Procter & Gamble and P&G are trade names of The Procter & Gamble Company and are used pursuant to an agreement with The Procter & Gamble Company. P&G Alumni Network is an independent organization apart from The Procter & Gamble Company.

Mission: As business professionals with the shared experience of having worked for Procter & Gamble, we have come together to serve our alumni around the world both personally and professionally and give back to society.

Vision: To harness the skills and talents of this group of people for both their personal growth and to the benefits of the communities in which we live and work and to become the most respected and most highly regarded business alumni organization in the world.

Goals – Purpose	Who We Serve	How We Will Serve	Action Plans and Measures		
			Near Term Emphasis		**Maintenance**
Facilitate connections between alumni for personal or professional contacts Measurement • Need to develop effective metrics for this goal.	Members	Members – Our goal is to serve all Procter alumni by connecting to and with alumni • Global Conferences • Communications • Sponsorship Opportunities • History & Values • Liaison with P&G	Membership • Grow membership globally Measurement • Number of new members each year, as well as total membership Communications • Update web site with new technology in 2014/15 • Increase utilization by members, chapters and global committees • Track hits and satisfaction; report regularly to the Board • Feedback on satisfaction with email frequency and content	Liaison with Procter & Gamble • Provide a single point of contact with the Company and maintain a positive but arms length working relationship • Retain and strengthen financial relationship with the Company Measurement • Track engagement with senior management • Track sponsorship	Global Conferences • Every two years, alternating geographies, chapter led with revenue sharing to the host; Women's Forum fully integrated into each event Measurement • Attendance • Satisfaction • Financial viability • Sponsor interest and satisfaction History and Values • Maintain Alumni Reflections Measurement • Track usage and satisfaction
	Chapters	Chapters – We will help existing chapters thrive and help new chapters to get established for the benefit of all alumni. • Best practices. • Start up funding – possible • Content/speaker resources • Sponsorship resources • Legal, Tax, Insurance resources	Chapters • Grow and support healthy chapters • Secure active leadership at the chapter and Region levels • Execute regular, periodic regional calls to encourage cooperation across regions Measurement • Number of new chapters each year, as well as total healthy chapters • Number of active Regional leaders • Regular reporting of regional meetings to the Board	Women's Forum • Establish a separate committee with the specific objective of integrating the Women's Forum into chapters Measurement • Establishment of the committee • Track interactions with chapters and regions • Report regularly to the Board	

Goals – Purpose	Who We Serve	How We Will Serve	Action Plans and Measures		
			Near Term Emphasis		**Maintenance**
Give back to the communities and organizations in which members are meaningfully involved	Philanthropic Beneficiaries in which our members are meaningfully involved	Three-Tiered Philanthropy – we will make our members proud to be a part of the Alumni Network by fulfilling our responsibility to society as a whole. • As a global Network with a focus on economic empowerment • And by harnessing our expertise for the benefit of third parties • Through our chapters via their own fund raising, expertise and manpower • Through individual members by facilitating their ability to work together.	Global Endowment • Hire Executive Director for Endowment program • Complete marketing campaign with Saatchi • Identify major donor targets • Develop and execute Endowment plan Measurement • Annual endowment funds raised against $25MM target • set goals and measure performance annually	Global Philanthropy • Broaden sources of funding and increase funding levels primarily through our speaker's bureau and webinars, secondarily through publications. Measurement • Annual global philanthropy • set goals and measure performance annually	Global Philanthropy • 501c3 – maintain IRS qualifications Measurement • Regular audits of processes
		Build the P&G Alumni Network brand by delivering on its promise in order to increase its inherent value for the organization and its members	Build Network brand through the selective proliferation of branded, high quality business materials and programs • Develop and execute more effective marketing of speakers bureau • Produce and execute new webinar program • Develop and execute effective marketing for webinar program Measurement • Track image of brand over time • Number and frequency of speaking events by country • Number, size and frequency of profitable seminars/conferences/webinars • Number and frequency of profitable publications		

Source: P&G Alumni Network. Used with permission

Vision: Become the category market share leader by investing in high ROI, growth-enhancing initiatives that create a superior consumer experience and establish our image as the Authority in XXX.			
Objective	Strategies	Measures	Tactics
Achieve Comp. Store Sales Increase of +2%	1. Deliver improved departmental performance via more consumer-centric insight, data-based analysis, and disciplined processes that inform program development, track progress, and measure performance.	All trackers executed Marketing Vehicle Analysis is completed and fund reallocation is approved Dashboards judged effective by CMO and CEO	METRICS: • Define metrics that we will measure performance by and hold ourselves accountable to (June). • Ensure that all programs developed have clearly written and aligned to objectives, goals, and measures before beginning implementation (immediately). DASHBOARDS: • Further enhance web, e-com, and vendor dashboards to enable quick identification of issues; ensure the dashboards sync up with overall program deliverables (July). • Develop a brand image dashboard that regularly measures functional and emotional attributes vs. importance and vs. competition (July). KEY PERFORMANCE AND ROI-ENHANCING ANALYSIS: • Marketing Vehicle Performance Analysis – Partner with Finance to determine a benchmark for cost/lead and value/lead to determine relative efficacy (Mar). • Marketing Program Performance – Conduct ROI analysis to assess marketing programs and reallocate funds based on insight; quantitatively test advertising against communication objectives (May).
	2. Further drive brand preference through identification and superior delivery on consumers' priority needs (i.e., improve the customer experience)	New brand proposition is superior vs. competitors and current; vision is approved by board Cost/lead = -5% versus YA Leads=+4% vs. YA	ENHANCE THE PROPOSITION and COMMUNICATION VEHICLES: • Elevate the brand by identifying and delivering a strategic, top-branded partner to co-develop product, promotion, and in-store experience (Dec). • Identify the most important category benefits and establish brand as being the authority in delivering them; concept test the current positioning and materials vs. potential evolutions vs. competition to ensure strongest position possible (Apr). • Develop and test "ideas" that can help lend credibility on how XXX better delivers the proposition (i.e., XXX, etc.) (Oct). • Pilot and measure more diverse/contemporary marketing media vehicles to distribute our brand messaging (ongoing). • Strengthen our media spend by driving a greater level of integration between vehicles (i.e., leverage print to drive the consumer to the web) (ongoing).
	3. Increase revenue performance via key innovations/initiatives that leverage the internet/web as the primary lead generation and conversion tool designed to increase revenue growth via key initiatives.	E-com/B2B revenue is greater than plan Leads +4% vs. YA Traffic +4% vs. YA Cost/lead and cost/customer -5% vs. YA Rev/customer generated from email program = +8% vs. YA	E-Com and B2B Business • Exceed the ecom plan by: (1) making it easier to "find" the shop, (2) increasing the assortment, and (3) opening our store to international orders (ongoing). • Ensure growth objective by deciding on and implementing a new technology platform that is scalable (December). • Resolve key issues regarding e-com integration with store business: (1) returns, and (2) commissions (June). • Increase B2B real estate to sell and develop new sales pitch to target mid-size companies (Mar). Internet/Web Program • Increase registration conversion by XXX via landing page tests, concept/creative tests, better click path management, and a backbone of stronger analytics (ongoing). • Optimize paid search by eliminating underperforming keywords (12% of dollars deliver 0 registrations) and/or improved click path management (ongoing). • Improve site conversion and consumer experience via a simpler, evolved design; thoroughly test to minimize risk (Sept). • Increase rev/customer by evolving e-mail to focus on behavior-changing vs. just relationship-enhancing efforts (ongoing). Store: Increase traffic to purchase conversion through improved store design, enhanced sales training program, improved store promotions, and additional financing options (e.g., store credit card, etc.) (ongoing).
	4. Enhance departmental performance via structure, rewards, and training that support stronger leadership and integration	Proposal for structure/rewards is agreed to Average performance ratings improve + 10%	• Structure: Work with HR to look at improving the org structure by moving from an execution-centric organization to a lead and integrate organization (proposal complete April). • Rewards: Work with HR to shift the paradigm from a followership mentality to a leadership, initiative, and ownership mentality; identify appropriate rewards to help support this shift (proposal complete April). • Coaching/Training: Work in a "hands on" capacity to provide daily coaching and development to enhance departmental performance over time (ongoing).

FIGURE AP 5.4 Strategic marketing plan example 2: P&G Alumni network

6

The Creative Brief

In my experience, the creative brief is the Rodney Dangerfield of business documents. . . . It gets no respect. Not because it isn't used. It is. The respect thing arises because the creative brief is so ubiquitous that it's taken for granted. It's part of the scenery and no one really sees it for its true value.

—HOWARD IBACH, *HOW TO WRITE AN INSPIRED CREATIVE BRIEF*[1]

Creatives . . . refuse to do advertising work for a product or service without a brief signed off by the client. Meanwhile, marketing people often fill out these briefs with the vaguest, most meaningless sentences possible that will make it impossible for the agency to blame them when the ads don't work.

—MARK DUFFY[2]

NOW THAT WE HAVE developed a strategic marketing plan, with strategies and tactics chosen that will help ensure that we achieve our objectives, how do we effectively activate the plan to achieve success? How are advertisements made? How are new products designed? How are social media campaigns created? And how do strategists effectively convey their vision, insight, and strategies to the teams of creatives that will execute—and ultimately determine the success of—the different communications? This chapter is designed to introduce the creative brief, a bridging document that plays a crucial role in converting strategy into action.

At one point in my time at Procter & Gamble (P&G), the firm sent me to Leo Burnett, a leading advertising firm, on a cross-training assignment. One of the benefits of working for a company known for great training is that they invest in such opportunities. From P&G's

point of view, the hope was that these experiences would enable their employees to better understand key stakeholders and therefore become better leaders. In this case, while I spent my time working as a creative (i.e., a copywriter), I had a very simple goal—to learn how to be a great client so that creatives would want to work on my business and I could be an effective strategic leader, enabling them to do their best work.

In this chapter, I will share insight so that you can avoid the mishaps that Duffy refers to. The creative brief tool and explanation about how to develop one effectively are designed to help you become a great strategic leader who can get an organization to effectively convert strategic plans into superior execution. While this chapter focuses on the creative brief, there are many similar documents (e.g., project briefs and technology briefs) that serve the same bridging purpose. As a result, this insight can be useful for creating any document that helps convert strategy into action.

What Is a Creative Brief?

The creative brief is a document written by strategists (generally brand managers/the client or planners within an agency) to communicate key information about a specific project so that the creatives have a guide or blueprint they can use to construct a marketing activity. It ultimately becomes an agreement between the marketers and creatives regarding the assignment, serving as the bridge between the strategic vision and the implementation of that vision, and is the mechanism through which the strategist's vision is communicated and converted into marketing programs (e.g., advertisements, events, brochures, magazines, in-store signage, sponsorship materials, and so forth).

The completed creative brief provides a map of the "who," "what," "where," "when," and "why" of a project. In most instances, those who spend hours listening to consumers, poring over data, and creating a brand strategy are different from those who create the marketing programs that present the brand directly to consumers; as a result, the creative brief is the primary conduit through which those who understand the consumer and brand transfer this knowledge to the people who create consumer-facing programs, and therefore can have a significant impact on whether the programs are relevant to the target, will change their beliefs and/or behaviors, and have a positive impact on the firm's results. While the right strategy can affect business outcomes, so can the way in which that strategy is implemented.

Who Uses a Creative Brief?

As a key mechanism for converting strategy into execution, the creative brief is a tool used nearly universally across industries and firms and can be used for any number of activities requiring creative development. Examples include advertisements (television, radio, print, online, and billboard), store design (signage, layout, and decor), brand-consumer communications (direct mail and email), website design, social media campaigns, events, logo design, and information technology (IT) projects.

Importantly, creative briefs can be designed for specific tactical executions (e.g., a specific ad) or can be created to span multiyear strategic communications platforms. The appendix at the end of the chapter includes the creative brief for a thinkThin campaign, which was used to develop a number of communication messages across a variety of marketing vehicles, including print and television. As such, creative briefs can be broader, such as for the thinkThin campaign, or narrower, such as for a single billboard.

Who Writes a Creative Brief?

While the individuals who write a creative brief can vary across firms, the decision is largely driven by the client's preferences.[3] For example,

McNeil Consumer Healthcare (the client) hired J. Walter Thompson (an advertising agency) to create an ad for Zyrtec (a specific product). The Zyrtec brand manager may choose to write the creative brief, ask the ad agency to write it, or write it with the agency.

The benefit of having people from the agency (i.e., account management or brand planning) write the brief is that they work within the same organization as the creatives who will ultimately craft the ad, so the communication is streamlined. However, this requires the agency to have greater insight into and connection to the business in order to be able to write an effective brief (see figure 6.1 for a visual representation of the client-agency structure). On the other hand, the benefit of having the client write the creative brief is that they often know more about the target consumer, the brand, and the business objectives; therefore, they should have deeper insight that can strengthen a creative brief. In many consumer package goods (CPG) firms, the client drafts the brief with input and feedback from agency partners; the final document thus represents a collaboration between the client and the agency. As such, it essentially becomes a cocreated document that establishes joint ownership of the project.

Another way that some marketers create mutual ownership is to write an assignment brief (the precursor to the creative brief) and

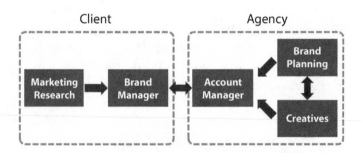

FIGURE 6.1 The client-agency relationship structure
*This is just one example of a structure. Some firms have an internal creative department, and other firms outsource much of the brand manager's work.

have the agency translate it into a creative brief. In the end, regardless of who writes the creative brief, it should have both agency and client input to make sure that it is as strong as possible and to establish joint responsibility.

When Do Companies Develop and Use a Creative Brief?

Historically, creative briefs are written after the firm has determined the corporate strategy, positioning concept, brand essence statement (BES), and strategic marketing plan (including market segmentation, targeting, and positioning). At this point, the brand (or firm) has decided on the direction it is going, and the brand strategists are ready to begin developing marketing communication messages (i.e., direct mail, advertising, billboards, digital ads, radio, social media campaigns, and so forth). As a result, the creative brief is really the first step in converting strategy into consumer-facing creative execution.

What Is Involved in the Creative Brief Development Process?

To begin the creative brief development process, the specific business objective must be defined. This flows from the strategic marketing plan and requires identifying the impact that the successful ad or campaign should have on the business. The business objective can be anything from generating awareness (e.g., unaided brand awareness) to growing share to building loyalty to increasing brand image ratings on specific attributes. Regardless of what business objective is chosen, devising it is the critical first step because it will define how the creative brief will connect to a specific business outcome.

Once the business objective is defined, it's time to define the communications objective (i.e., the primary message that the creative should convey to the target audience) and to start writing the creative brief, which requires both depth of insight and strategic focus. The point of the creative brief is to express, on paper, the strategic direction behind the ad or campaign that should motivate the target audience to take a desired action (e.g., in the case of a CPG company, to purchase a product, or in the case of a nonprofit, to make a donation or volunteer). To do this, the client and agency partner must generate deep insight regarding the consumer. This includes some or all of the following: (1) conducting primary research (e.g., market research) via quantitative research (e.g., surveys) and qualitative research (e.g., ethnographies); (2) using secondary data (e.g., census data) when available; and (3) using behavioral and other types of first-party data such as purchase data and web browsing behavior.

In the example shown in figure 6.2, the business objective is presumably to increase market share by attracting new customers and building greater loyalty among existing customers. The communication

FIGURE 6.2 Mr. Clean ad

objective reinforces the primary benefit of buying and using Mr. Clean—whitening. The ad quickly and effectively demonstrates the primary rational benefit (i.e., the excellent whitening/cleaning ability) of Mr. Clean. Notice that the whitening demonstration took place under the harshest of circumstances, communicating not just good, but *excellent* whitening/cleaning ability. To communicate exceptional performance, the creatives used a road exposed to heavy traffic and inclement weather—arguably impossible conditions under which to keep something clean or white. It is likely that the rational benefit expressed in the BES required that the brand communication demonstrate proof of *superior* cleaning/whitening performance. Research with consumers likely helped the brand team identify a series of tough scenarios—gold standard circumstances—that only the best whitening product could successfully clean. In the aggregate, this example demonstrates how the BES and consumer insight, when communicated through a creative brief, can help lead creatives to develop powerful and persuasive work that is on strategy. What is notable is that this ad conveyed a clear BES without any words.

But converting all the information from the previous chapters into a focused creative brief is easier said than done. Most companies (especially those who communicate in short-length media vehicles, such as thirty-second television or radio spots) will focus on a single-minded message. In contrast, companies advertising via infomercials or direct response television (DRTV) will often use multiple messages in their communication strategy. Imagine writing a brief for a new store design for Walmart, a new Nordstrom catalog, or helping a business-to-business (B2B) firm (e.g., Oracle or Salesforce.com) in their effort to acquire new customers through thought leadership (e.g., content-based programs). Creative briefs will vary depending on a number of factors, such as the brand, business objective, competition, and communication vehicle (e.g., social, mobile, print, and television). However, the clearer the brief is about the primary message being communicated, the greater the likelihood that the target audience will understand the main idea.

The Seven Elements of a Creative Brief

Because there are so many contributing factors, no two creative briefs are alike. Companies and ad agencies often have a preferred format that tends to include most or all of the elements listed here. See the appendix for examples of completed briefs and the resulting ads.

Project Assignment. This section of the creative brief summarizes the overall task and project deliverables. The more specificity, the better.

For example: Create a thirty-second advertising campaign (comprising three commercials) to launch Lender's new frozen "New York Style" line of bagels, designed to reinvigorate the Lender's brand.[4]

Project Background/Situation. This section details the opportunity or problem that the creative execution is designed to address. Why is this project being done, and what relevant background information do the creatives need to create a successful campaign?

For example: Lender's was the first to introduce bagels to the United States, and to many consumers, the brand is synonymous with the category (i.e., Lender's = bagels). However, the frozen line of products has declined (volume down 5 percent compared to a year ago), and in recent research among bagel enthusiasts (i.e., those purchasing more than twelve bags of bagels a year), Lender's frozen products are not as compelling to bagel consumers who specifically prefer traditional, large, New York–style bagels.

Project Objective and Success Criteria. What are the goals of the project? What are you hoping to accomplish, and how will this be measured? This section must focus on the measures that the project has a legitimate possibility of affecting. For example, notice that in the Lender's example, the objective is not to improve the overall brand image. That is because it is unlikely that a single ad campaign focused on the chosen attributes (taste, authenticity, and innovation) would lead to an improvement in the overall brand image. Instead, the objective is to improve the brand's ratings in ad testing on these

128

three specific attributes, consistent with the message being created and delivered.

For example: This new product should generate 100,000 incremental cases of frozen bagels. Further, we expect this campaign to deliver a statistically significant improvement (year over year) in Lender's advertising testing metrics on the following attributes: "is a New York bagel," "is the best-tasting bagel," and "is a real, authentic bagel." We will test the creative executions in copy testing, and it must beat our current advertising on overall purchase intent and the three attributes.

Identify Target and Deep Consumer Insight. It is critical to convey who the target is and the deep insight that connects the consumer's need/want/desire to the solution that the brand provides. Without this understanding, it isn't possible to create an ad that is anchored on the consumer—instead, the ad will be based on the product or service. And this is a mistake. Great marketing starts by being "market (or customer) oriented" and connects the dots between the consumer's need and the brand's solution. Further, it is possible (and in many cases likely) that the creative brief is the only background information and insight that the creatives will have about the consumer. The greater the precision and depth of insight, the better.

For example: The target group is female heads of household, age twenty-five to forty-nine years old (with an emphasis on thirty-four to forty-four), with kids age six to seventeen (with an emphasis on kids thirteen to seventeen). Among the target, Lender's is perceived to be a trustworthy brand and excellent value. Bagels are a staple among these households due to their ease (kids and moms can make them quickly), flexibility (they can be used to make a number of different meals and snacks) and value (they have a lower price than a lot of other breakfast and snack options). However, some in the target group believe that the size of Lender's frozen bagels makes them inferior to traditional bagels found in New York. The new "New York Style" bagels have been designed to deliver fresh bagel taste, but with the convenience of being frozen.

Communications Strategy. This section is designed to convey the key message; specifically, it includes the consumer benefit (i.e., what the brand can do for the consumer) that addresses the problem stated in the "Identify Target and Deep Consumer Insight" section. By stating the brand benefit, this section helps illuminate what the consumer should think and/or feel. Some briefs emphasize the elements related to the BES (e.g., the benefit, the reason to believe, and the tone). Others will choose to focus on the behavior desired from the consumer (see the Lender's example). Some will emphasize the most important single thing to communicate (to keep it simple and focused). Regardless, the communications strategy for any specific creative brief should flow from, and fit with, your BES. Note that the writing of a creative brief is not necessarily consumer friendly, given that it is designed to be strategic in nature; however, while not to the level of creative-quality writing, the strategist will still want to capture key words and phrases that are relevant to the target and strategy (e.g., "fresh-out-of-the-oven taste").

For example: Here is the solution to the problem identified in the "Identify Target and Deep Consumer Insight" section: Lender's new "New York Style" frozen bagels, which "lock in" flavor at the peak of freshness, have a "fresh-out-of-the-oven" taste that's just like what you would find in a New York deli.

The communication strategy will focus on creating a desire for "New York Style Bagels," communicating that Lender's New York Style Bagels are superior.

For reference, here is the brand strategy (from the BES): Introducing new Lender's "New York Style" bagels that are so good, they taste like they're fresh-out-of-the-oven.

Support:

1. They're larger: Like most things in the Big Apple, they are jumbo-sized.
2. Lender's unique fresh lock system "locks in" the flavor and freshness right out of the oven: So when you toast or microwave the bagel (which releases the flavor), you can be guaranteed that it will have that "just baked" taste and fresh texture.

3. Big, New York flavor: They're tasty and packed with real, flavor-filled ingredients such as wild Maine blueberries and sun-ripened California raisins. Even Lender's plain bagel is packed with flavor because it is made with sea salt butter from Vermont.

4. In blind taste tests, consumers rate Lender's new bagels as superior to the best-selling bagel stocked in the bread aisle for "freshness," "flavor," and "taste."

Executional Guidelines/Mandatory Elements. In this section, you want to outline any mandatory elements, including brand elements, legal and regulatory requirements (e.g., disclaimers), URL, pricing, or promotion details.

For example: Use the new brand logo; include a visual of a bag of New York Style bagels (comp quality bag); include the URL. Make sure to convey the brand voice (or personality from the BES).

Details and Approvals. In this section, some brands will include details about the delivery, distribution, and approvals that will be required. Who needs to sign off on the creative brief before work begins? This depends on the client and agency norms.

For example: In the case of the hypothetical Lender's example, the CMO will sign off on the campaign.

Key Principles of Developing a Strong Creative Brief

There are five important aspects to consider when developing the creative brief, regardless of the firm or industry:

1. **Have a transparent process.** While the process for developing a creative brief varies across firms, it's essential to be as transparent as possible with all stakeholders regarding the steps required. What is the role of consumer insight? How is this

converted into a brief? Who is involved in translating consumer insight and business needs into a brief? Who approves the final document prior to the creatives being assigned to the project? If the brief is unclear, what can the creatives do to ensure clarity (i.e., feedback loops)? What happens if the creatives don't agree with the brief? Without clarity and transparency regarding the process, the possibility of frustration, confusion, and rework exists.

2. **Have a clear owner.** While many stakeholders may be involved, it is important to have one individual who is responsible for managing the document sign-off process (in some firms, this person is called the "trafficker;" in other firms, it may be an account manager) and for the content of the document (e.g., the marketing director). The person responsible for the content should understand how difficult it is to create great advertising and have appropriate respect for the role of creatives. He or she should be a good thinker, writer, and collaborator and should have good judgment and competency in developing focused strategic plans.

3. **Involve all key stakeholders.** It's best to involve key stakeholders early in the process rather than waiting until the brief has been approved. This includes the creatives. Aligning all key stakeholders up front on the expectations, deliverables, and measurement will increase the odds of success later.

4. **Remember that you are *not* the target.** This point is one of the hardest things for clients and creatives alike to remember. The ad is not being developed for you, even if you are part of the target consumer group. For example, if you are a mother of two working on an ad for Downy (and you perfectly represent both the demographic and psychographic targets), you must work extra hard to focus on the needs of the entire target group, not yourself. It's critical to stay focused on what the generalizable insights suggest about the entire group. As a result, it's often easier to work on brands where

you are not the target because it forces you to go beyond your own beliefs, experiences, and expectations to learn about the actual target.

5. **Base the brief on consumer insight.** The deeper the consumer understanding, the richer the insight and the more likely the brand is to connect with the target consumer in a meaningful way that changes beliefs and behavior. Dove's "Campaign for Real Beauty" is based on an insight that, in retrospect, seems obvious. Through research, Dove's brand leaders discovered that the images, ads, and magazines touting perfect (i.e., airbrushed) women actually become a source of anxiety. Globally, only 2 percent of women described themselves as beautiful. With this in mind, Dove envisioned "a world where beauty is a source of confidence, not anxiety"[5] and launched a new campaign in 2004 designed to broaden the definition of beauty, empower women, and provide a source of confidence to them. What was the impact? The first videos created received over 35 million views each—within the first two weeks of being uploaded to YouTube—and one ad received unpaid exposure estimated to be worth over $150 million.[6]

How to Be a Great Client

Because the collaboration between the ad agency and the firm is so important, it is crucial to develop a strong, healthy working relationship. Talk to any creative, and they will share story after story of difficult, misleading, and micromanaging clients. As a strategist, part of your job is not only to create clear guidelines for the creatives, but to actually help inspire and motivate them to deliver breakthrough work. How much time, energy, and passion the creatives put into the work is often a reflection of the joy that they get from working on the project with the client. Remember that creatives will be managing multiple projects at once, so where they invest their energy is within their control. As mentioned at the beginning of the chapter, P&G historically sent employees to work at advertising agencies prior to becoming brand managers. The logic was that they wanted strategic leaders to understand what it was like to be on the other side of the table, sitting in the seats of the creatives. The more brand managers understood the creatives' challenge, they argued, the better the brand managers would be at effectively inspiring creatives to achieve breakthrough results. Whether marketers have an internal or external agency partner, the following outlines some attributes of *great*—not good—clients:

1. **Focus first on developing a trust-based partnership.** Great creative output is usually the result of a great partnership based on trust, respect, and a shared commitment to the objectives. While this may seem obvious, it is not always easy to achieve. Creatives may be working on several projects with different clients and thus not necessarily focused on one specific brand. The brand team, in contrast, may spend all day thinking about only one brand. Strategists, brand managers, and creatives have different skills, working styles, and affinities. But the more aligned the client and agency are on the objectives and the greater the degree of trust, the stronger the foundation from which the creative output can be developed.

2. **Emphasize the objective, not the tactic.** One of the biggest mistakes that clients/strategists make is critiquing the tactic rather than focusing on the objective. For example, imagine that you are the marketing manager for Downy fabric softener, and part of the stated brand personality in the creative brief (from the BES) is that the brand represents warmth, human connection, and the loving touch of a mother. The agency then presents a creative execution with a lot of cool colors and individuals that don't show any human connection. A less effective way to provide feedback is to say, "I don't like the colors in the ad. We should have more reds."

This critique is anchored in tactical execution elements rather than the stated objective. A more effective way to provide feedback is to say: "The brand personality is one of warmth, human connection, and the loving touch of a mother. I don't believe the current execution delivers on this as well as it could. I would like to see the execution better reflect the brand's personality." The creatives may come back and ask you why you believe that it doesn't reflect the brand personality, and you should be able to explain your thinking. And they may disagree with your point of view and explain why the ad actually delivers the brand personality. The key here is to focus on a strategic objective (i.e., delivering the brand personality) and leave the "how" up to the creatives.

3. **Ask questions and seek to understand the creatives.** Related to the previous point, a lot of the interaction should be anchored on seeking to understand the creatives' perspective. One of the more inspirational tools for creatives is to have engaged discussions—on a strategic level—about the creative execution. The creatives have invested a lot in time and effort trying to develop breakthrough advertising. By deeply engaging with them on a strategic level, asking questions and being curious about their work, you are showing respect. An even better way to provide feedback in the previous example is to say the following: "As you know, the brand personality is one of warmth, human connection, and the loving touch of a mother. Can you please help me understand how you think the current execution delivers on this?" Another way of approaching this could be to say: "Tell me more about how we're achieving the objective. Help me understand your thinking." By asking questions, you allow a deeper, more thought-provoking conversation to emerge that engages everyone in the room. In many cases, the creatives have a very good reason for their choice of colors that the strategists may not see. By failing to understand the creatives' rationale, the strategists

could miss an even bigger point. Ultimately, the more deeply everyone engages in the process, the greater the likelihood that you will get compelling work from the creatives.

4. **Don't dictate solutions, but rather provide guidance.** There is a strong likelihood that the creatives have a very good reason for ignoring the brand personality when developing the creative execution. There may be conflicting elements of the creative brief that cause the creatives to prioritize one communication element over another, they may have interpreted the brief differently, or they may have executed the communication element in a different, subtler way. When you agree that there should be an evolution in the creative process, focus on providing objective-based guidance rather than dictating a solution. By using this approach, it is easier to foster a nondefensive discussion that can lead to better engagement and results. Just as you want the latitude to manage the specifics of your job, you'll want to give the creatives freedom to solve their problems. After all, the creatives may come up with something that you hadn't considered, which is what they are good at.

5. **React to creative executions first as a human being, and then as a strategist.** P&G famously trains marketers to *feel* a creative execution before *thinking* about it. This is difficult to do and takes a lot of practice. After viewing an ad, how does it make you feel? And then, how well does it deliver on the creative brief? Once you have figured out how you feel and think, communicate this to the creatives. To provide an example of this approach, I once saw a general manager view an advertising campaign and say, "I've been told that creatives prefer it if we react to advertising as a real person. Well, I'm not going to sugarcoat it. I hate it." He then told them why and anchored his rationale on both his emotional reaction and a logical discussion of how the work didn't deliver on the creative brief. It's easy to say that you want real emotional feedback, but it can sting when the feedback is negative. After that meeting,

I talked with the agency representatives, and they actually said they appreciated the honest feedback. It's often hard to tell how bad or good an ad is when strategists provide feedback in the same manner and tone for every ad. By being clear about his emotional reaction, the general manager actually provided greater clarity and direction.

6. **"Major on the major"**. It's easy to pick apart a creative execution. What's hard is understanding what really matters. After reviewing an ad, it's possible to identify a number of areas where the ad could be strengthened to deliver on the creative brief. But the strategist's job is to know which of these myriad improvements matter and which don't, and which will have a meaningful impact on consumer behavior and which won't. By asking creatives to focus on one or two primary issues as opposed to a number of tactical improvements, you have a better chance of getting both high-quality work and a creative execution that delivers on the most important objectives.

Converting a Creative Brief into a Creative Execution

How is a creative brief converted into a creative execution? The following box shows an example of a creative brief for Mastercard's (MC's) famous campaign regarding life's most important moments and the final advertising for a very successful advertising campaign.

Mastercard's (MC's) "Priceless" Campaign Creative Brief

Project: Create an integrated campaign, including: TV (0:30 and 0:60), radio (0:30 and 0:60), out-of-home (billboard), and print (full-page and two-page spread).
Business Challenge: While MC has nearly the same awareness level of VISA, MC lags VISA in ownership and frequency of usage. Further,

VISA has had a consistent campaign for years, while MC has changed advertising campaigns multiple times over the past decade. Consumer research indicates that MC's image is unclear (no distinct personality beyond the functional benefit of being accepted everywhere) and is negatively affecting MC's share (declining over the past few years). Given MC's strong penetration (high percentage of credit card users who have MC), the primary business opportunity is to convince MC users to use their MCs for daily necessities.

Campaign Purpose: To change consumer behavior. In addition to increasing usage among current MC credit card holders, this campaign must elevate the MC brand beyond functional messaging, connecting with consumers on an emotional level, and therefore creating a differentiated position relative to VISA.

Campaign Goal: Increase the frequency of MC use occasions by XXX percent.

Target Insight:

Target: MC users who carry multiple cards, don't see a difference between cards, and tend to use cash for everyday purchases. They tend to use credit cards for credit rather than as an alternative to cash purchases.

Consumer Mindset: "While many people tend to be defined by their purse or their car, I'm different because I know that material wealth doesn't bring happiness. What really matters in life are the moments that you can't buy, like your child's first word or a puppy's tail wag. Life's greatest moments are about more than money, possessions, and stuff."

Communication Strategy:

Benefit: MC is the only card you depend on for everyday purchases (rational benefit) so that you can enjoy life's most important moments (emotional benefit).

Reason to Believe: That's because MC is more convenient because it is universally accepted.

Brand Personality: MC is the better you, your conscience, which consistently reminds you of what really matters in life.

(Created by author by reviewing a number of sources and reverse engineering the Creative Brief from the advertising.[7])

Why the Mastercard Campaign Is a Breakthrough

Once you have read this creative brief example, view an original Mastercard ad to see how the brief influenced the creative development process and output.[8]

At the heart of a great creative brief is great consumer insight. That insight, combined with creative genius, can be converted into a campaign (not just one ad, but a series of ads) that distinguishes one brand from its competitors (e.g., VISA and American Express) and is memorable and compelling. This is not an easy feat. The Mastercard execution was centered on a core value—the idea that life's most meaningful moments are about human connection, not material things. At face value, it might seem odd that a credit card company would highlight this value. But by associating Mastercard with this core belief, the strategy enabled the brand to rise above the functional attributes of a credit card and stand for positive, aspirational experiences. As a result, Mastercard was able to transcend a simple rational benefit (universal acceptance) by providing an emotional benefit and context through which the brand can effectively connect with consumers and deliver critical messages.

In addition, Mastercard had a very clear understanding of what consumer behavior it wanted to change (i.e., the business challenge)— the usage patterns of Mastercard consumers. The executions consistently reinforced using the credit card for life's big and small purchases, visually demonstrating how to use the card everywhere. Importantly, the ad didn't just differentiate the brand—it changed consumer behavior that led to better business results.

As the Mastercard example illustrates, an element of a great creative brief is that it sets a standard above which the creatives must deliver. Howard Ibach told the story of a creative director at a top London ad agency who essentially said that the creative brief is the first ad in the campaign, and it is the creative's job to create something better.[9] As you write a creative brief, are you setting the standard high enough?

Without great strategic thinking communicated via the creative brief, it is unlikely that you will get an inspired creative product. And this is an important part of the creative brief. Imagine if the Mastercard creative brief had said that the consumer insight was centered on the fact that consumers didn't regularly use their credit cards? What if the consumer insight about what mattered most in life wasn't on the creative brief? What type of campaign might have been created? Most likely, not the award-winning, breakthrough campaign that we just saw.

Summary

Creating great strategic direction is important. But if it isn't converted into stellar creative work, it can lead to subpar results. And yet, despite the tremendous amount of time that firms spend on determining the optimal strategy, the most important document that determines whether a strategic plan will be effective often fails to receive enough attention and effort. Part of the challenge here is that the creatives have to convert a short document into creative genius that changes consumer behavior. Imagine being responsible for creating a thirty-second ad that has to change how consumers think, feel, or behave. This is exceptionally hard. The more time that strategists invest up front to make the brief as persuasive and clear as possible, the easier you are making the creatives' job and the greater the likelihood that you will get breakthrough creative output.

Appendix

Background	Why you are doing this. (It may seem obvious, but it helps to put it down on paper.) This is the business background, what the company is, what the business goals are, competitive environment, opportunities spotted in the marketplace, etc. Write it simply and clearly — as if to a ten-year-old.
Objective	What **this particular piece** of promotional material should achieve.
Target Audience	Define them as people, not just job title. Their age, background, what their daily concerns are.
Promise	What you are offering them in a **single sentence**. (This is not a description of your product or service, it's how it will benefit the reader.)
Support for Your Promise	The features and details of your product or service which back up the main benefit in your promise. This can be as long as you like — the more information the better.
Key Message	What the readers should think, feel, and **DO** as a result of reading this.
Timing and Parameters	What format, size, etc. it is and when it's required.

FIGURE AP 6.1 Creative brief format example 1

Project Sponsor:		Due Date:	
To:		Job Number:	
CC:		Budget:	
		GL Code (to change costs):	

Project Title / Summary
Name the project. What deliverables do we need from the creative team (e.g., catalog, brochure, direct mail, store signage, web shoot, and image request)?

Project Overview
What are your goals? What is the opportunity or problem that the creative team must address? What is the background of the project? Why is this project being done?

Project Objective
What are you trying to achieve? A concise statement of the effect the deliverable should have on consumers. What do you want our customer to think, feel, or do?

Communications Strategy
Introduce the product to creative; what is the key message or single most important thing to say to achieve the objective? Are there secondary messages? What is the desired perception and benefit? What tone and imagery should we use to engage the target?

Executional Guidelines / Mandatory Elements
What are the offers, size, legal disclaimers, vendor logo, address, phone number, web address, and coupon codes?

Reference Materials

Measurement / Success Criteria
What will we measure and how will we measure results?

Quantity / Distribution / Delivery Information

Approvals
Who needs to sign off on final execution?

FIGURE AP 6.2 Creative brief format example 2

Timing	Audience	Deliverables	Mandatories

The Business Barrier (what problem are we solving?)

The Tangible Business Goal (what is the desired outcome of this advertising?)

Consumer Insight	Reasons to Believe (why?)

Single-Minded Message

FIGURE AP 6.3 Creative brief format example 3

Send Broadcast Requests to:
Send Print Requests to:

Please fill out completely in order to expedite your request. Attach any related documents. Allow 10 days for development; fully produced creative will take longer. In addition, Legal requires 5 days for approval.

DATE SUBMITTED:
CONTACT INFORMATION:
  Name: Email: Region/Department:
  Phone Number: Fax:

BRAND:
TITLE OF CREATIVE:
MARKET(S) WHERE CREATIVE WILL RUN:

TARGET AUDIENCE:

COMMUNICATION OBJECTIVE: (What message do you want delivered to consumers?)

BUSINESS OBJECTIVE: (Reason for advertising need? Could this be accomplished without advertising? What is the business risk of not doing this advertising?)

FLIGHT PERIOD/PUBLICATION DATE/POSTING DATE: From: _____ To:
_____

PRODUCTION BUDGET:
MEDIA BUDGET SOURCE: □ Paid media   □ Bartered   □ Other
IF A PROMOTION/MEDIA MERCHANDISING: (Please list all details of the promotion, method of entry, station/retail partner to be included, etc.)
ADDITIONAL NOTES: (Please list partner logos required and/or footage available for creative development)

PRINT AD REQUEST

MATERIALS DUE TO PUB/OOH COMPANY: _____
Format: □ Newspaper   □ Magazine   □ OOH   □ Web   □ Other
Color: □ 4C   □ BW
Dimensions: (Please indicate all sizes needed.) _____
Publication information: (Please attach spec sheet if available.)
Contact:
Phone:
Address:
Final format of ad to be sent:

BROADCAST AD REQUEST

CREATIVE (script/board) DUE TO STATION FOR LOCAL PRODUCTION BY:
□ Agency Produced   □ Locally Produced
Format: □ Television   □ 0:60   □ 0:30   □ 0:10 Tag
            □ Radio scripts □ 0:60   □ 0:40   □ 0:30
            □ Radio tags   □ 0:20   □ 0:10

FIGURE AP 6.4 Creative brief format example 4
Source: Adapted from Mel Henson (2011), "How to Write a Creative Brief that Gets Results," *SmartInsights*, [available at: http://www.smartinsights.com/digital-marketing-strategy/creative-brief-template/].

Completed Creative Briefs

Objective:	Launch thinkThin communications across all media under a new, unified brand idea and look/tone/feel in order to significantly raise awareness among consumers—while also raising excitement among retailers.
Context:	thinkThin is a premium protein bar brand, marketed mainly to women, founded by former fashion model Lizanne Falsetto in 2000. In that time, thinkThin has grown to include national distribution and multiple SKUs. thinkThin was recently acquired by TSG Consumer Partners with the goal of growing the business significantly in the coming years.
Status Quo:	(The conventions that drive the category) ***The energy bar category is a "rainbow of confusion" that leads to "bar hopping."*** With so many brands and so many ingredient and form variations available to consumers, there is very little loyalty. Brands are generally playing in the same space, listing quality ingredients and expecting consumers to understand the benefits.
High Ground:	(The whitespace we can own) ***thinkThin is a champion for women and their nutrition.*** If we can prove that we are a brand that empowers women to be their best selves, through nutrition, positivity, and an active lifestyle, we can transcend the category and own a powerful place in the lives of women. To do so, we must actively take on anyone that deprives women of living life to the fullest, and anyone that limits their sense of self-image and self-worth.
Elevation:	(How we'll reach the high ground.) ***Inspire women to think positively about themselves and what they eat.*** Everything we do, from the energy we provide, to our ingredients, to our products, to our marketing messages, will inspire women to live life to the fullest. And we will take on anyone that gets in the way of that mission.
Tagline:	thinkPositive.
Product Reason to Believe:	Delicious, high-quality protein that delivers energy anytime, anywhere.
Brand Reasons to Believe:	TBD; our actions and the way we message and market. Lizanne's personal mission is to inspire women to live their best lives.
Brand Character:	We see ourselves as The Heroine, seeking to help women triumph over a system that makes them feel self-conscious about their nutrition, weight, and image. We do this with confidence, competence, faith, optimism, and positivity.
Consumer:	Women who want to feel good about themselves, the choices they make, and the brands

FIGURE AP 6.5 Example of completed creative brief for thinkThin

Deliverables:	-Tagline
	-Manifesto
	-Launch TV commercial
	-15-second video pre-roll
	-Print ad example
	-Outdoor board example
	-FSI example
	-Banner ad example
	-Example homepage refresh
	-Example Facebook refresh
	-Example Facebook Posts
	-Example Twitter Posts
	-News/buzzworthy, non-traditional idea
	-Philanthropy idea
	-PR idea
	-Campaign look/tone/feel that unites all of the above
Executional considerations:	
	-Use newly approved logo
	-Leverage new packaging cues from Landor
	-Consider CTA's "Look for us in the energy bar aisle."
	-Must extend to specific product communications/launches
	-Maintain premium look/tone/feel
	-Consider "NEW"-ness of Lean Bar for "introducing" language.

FIGURE AP 6.5 (cont'd)

To see how this Creative Brief converted into advertising, see the print ad below and the TV commercial located at: https://www.youtube.com/watch?v=u29xtcbckq4, or look up ThinkThin "Runner" commercial if the link is broken.

Source: Creative Brief and ad provided by Michele Kessler (Darden School of Business MBA '89), former president of thinkThin.

Guilt free.
Unless you steal one.

20 grams of protein. 0 grams of sugar. 0 guilt. **think**Thin. **think**Positive.

Look for us in the energy bar aisle.

FIGURE AP 6.6 Example of ad created from the thinkThin creative brief in figure Ap 6.1

Everyday Moments

Brand Essence:
The allergy "life" saver

Brand Promise:
Benadryl recognizes that everyone deserves to enjoy all of the special moments that make life fulfilling. That's why Benadryl provides failsafe relief to allergy sufferers so they can keep experiencing those moments.

Insight:
My allergies can be unpredictable. When they strike, it's frustrating because the symptoms cause me to cut short my enjoyment of life's everyday moments; especially those times shared with friends or family. I want to stay in the moment. I need something I can count on unequivocally to provide fast, effective relief regardless of how bad the allergens are, or how bad my symptoms are.

Benefit:
Benadryl provides **superior allergy relief** so you won't have to cut short your enjoyment of everyday moments.

RTB:
Benadryl is **more effective than the leading allergy medicine** at relieving your worst symptoms like runny nose, sneezing, and watery eyes.

Personality:
They're always there when I need them, know exactly what I need, "get" me, they empower me, **they're a complete "life"-saver.**

FIGURE AP 6.7 Example of completed creative brief for Benadryl
Source: Creative Brief and ad provided by Angela Li (Darden School of Business MBA '03) from Johnson & Johnson. BENADRYL is an equity of McNeil Consumer Healthcare Division, Johnson & Johnson Consumer, Inc. Used with permission.

FIGURE AP 6.8 Example of ad created from the Benadryl creative brief in figure Ap 6.2

Brand Proposition	Tango is a Sleeping Giant
What do we need to do?	Increase sales 1) Re-inform people of our traditional brand values 2) Re-engage people 3) Generate key interest in the product
What are the Market Insights?	The carbonated drink market is in decline. Few brands are surviving, and those that are still suffer a drop in sales. This is because the media is making health a real issue. Tango has always been a controversial brand. It stands out, makes a statement, and stands for something. Sadly, in recent years, this controversial stance has somewhat lessened. They've gone a bit soft with Tango Clear. We need to assert what we are in order to shake up the market and reclaim our prime position.
What are the Consumer Insights?	Stuck in an in-between state, teenagers associate themselves with the products and brands they consume. They take on a brand's personality as a representation of their own. Therefore, if a brand has no personality, it's impossible for them to feel an affiliation toward it. Tango is definitely a brand with a personality; however, it isn't currently being asserted. In order to gain a loyal consumer base, we need to give teenagers something that's worth being involved with.
What is the single most important thing to say?	JOIN THE TANGO RESISTANCE.
Reasons to Believe	Tango is not your ordinary drink; it says something about you. It's controversial, daring, and overt. This isn't just a carbonated drink. It's your chance to take a stance against all of the things that hold you back.
What do we want teenagers to do?	Get excited about the Tango revolution and join the resistance.
What do we want teenagers think/feel?	Think – "Tango understands us." Feel – More inclined to drink Tango on a regular basis as it's about more than just a carbonated drink.
Why would they bother?	This is about them. It empowers teenagers and gives them a voice.
What worked last time?	Tango enjoyed the most success when it was assertive about what it stands for.
Where will this appear?	Integrated campaign with a particular concentration on online as this is where our audience spends most of their time.
Inspirations	Think about what you were like at 16.

FIGURE AP 6.9 Tango creative brief.
Source: Adapted from Howard Ibach (2009), *How to Write an Inspired Creative Brief*, USA: iUniverse.

MARKETING PLAN TOOLS

7

The Marketing Technology Blueprint

There was 5 Exabytes of information created between the dawn of civilization through 2003, but that much information is now created every 2 days, and the pace is increasing.
—ERIC SCHMIDT, CHAIR OF GOOGLE[1]

Marketing is now a Technical Discipline. . . . We expect technology spend by CMOs to increase 10x in 10 years, from $12 billion to $120 billion, unlocking a huge opportunity for marketing technology companies and opening the door to the Decade of the CMO.
—ASHU GARG, GENERAL PARTNER, FOUNDATION CAPITAL[2]

UP TO THIS POINT, the emphasis of this book has been on creating a superior strategic position, reflecting the positioning concept in the brand essence statement (BES), and using the strategic planning and creative brief tools to help bridge the strategy-implementation divide. The next stage in the marketing impact framework discussed in chapter 1 is to implement the strategic marketing plan. While there are innumerable ways that marketers can achieve key strategic objectives, I focus here on three contemporary planning tools that (1) are newer and more relevant; (2) have less coverage in academic and popular press publications; and (3) are generally important to marketers across firms and industries and therefore, more universally relevant. However, while I cover only three tools, my hope is that by the time you are done reading, you will begin thinking like an artisan and use this acquired knowledge to begin building your own tools.

In this chapter, I describe the Marketing Technology (MarTech) Blueprint, a tool designed to integrate marketing activities, technology, and the consumer experience in a simple map to help aid in decision-making. In chapter 8, I provide an influencer mapping tool to help marketers ensure that their influencer programs connect with their strategies. And in chapter 9, I provide a framework for how to think about measuring brands.

Why the MarTech Blueprint Is Useful

Today's consumers have access to and are armed with powerful technology that makes them more connected, informed, and pickier about the brands and companies with which they conduct business. Case in point—just twenty years ago, consumers would have to drive from store to store to learn about and compare products, prices, and features. Today, we can do more—and faster—with our smartphones and a few mobile apps than a team of research scientists could do just a decade ago.[3]

To meet this new customer reality, chief marketing officers (CMOs) are spearheading the investment of billions of dollars in technology to help modernize marketing in an effort to discover, engage, create, and delight customers (in the most cost-efficient way possible). Not only do marketers want to know what consumers like and dislike, how they behave, and where they are located, they want to translate this insight into differentiated products, services, and experiences that distinguish their firms from competitors and create meaningful value for customers.

The gold rush for identifying and deploying new technology is on. And, accordingly, so is the wide array of marketing technologies and providers ready to sell them to CMOs. With over 7,000 MarTech providers,[4] the explosion of marketing solutions presents vast opportunities while making the identification of the *right* MarTech investments a daunting process. And that's just trying to identify the right investments and partners. The key question that CMOs are seeking to answer is: "How can technology be leveraged across the enterprise to create superior value for consumers?"

With the increased investment in MarTech, marketers are making critical decisions related to what technology to purchase and from whom to purchase it.[5] But with the increased tech responsibility and budgets, marketing executives must effectively evaluate the ways that new technologies will work with existing processes. How can technology integrate a firm's existing infrastructure with new solutions to create and deliver superior consumer experiences (creating consumer value that ultimately leads to firm value)? How can different sources of data (e.g., point of purchase, scanner, secondary sources, surveys, websites, searches, and social media) be combined to provide holistic insight on the business? What could the future consumer experience be—and how might technology enable it? The number of potential solutions makes the identification, integration, and management of technology-based solutions among the most difficult marketing challenges.

Few CMOs are technologists. Yet they are at the center of the process needed to define, specify, resource, integrate, and implement technology-enabled marketing solutions. This is where CMOs and marketing teams can turn to the MarTech Blueprint tool. See figure 7.1 for an example of the complexity of the MarTech landscape.

What Is the MarTech Blueprint?

With increasing amounts of capital being invested in technology and so much at stake for marketers and the brands they represent, marketers need a tool to help them make smarter decisions about MarTech investments and then communicate and sell these ideas across the enterprise. The MarTech Blueprint is a tool used for evaluating, informing, and supporting MarTech investment across an entire organization.

The starting point for many of the tools described in the book, you may have noticed, is similar to that of constructing a building—modernizing marketing with technology starts with smart architecture and a solid blueprint. In this case, the MarTech Blueprint is a diagram or visual representation that illustrates how technologies connect and work with each other to drive all or

April 2018

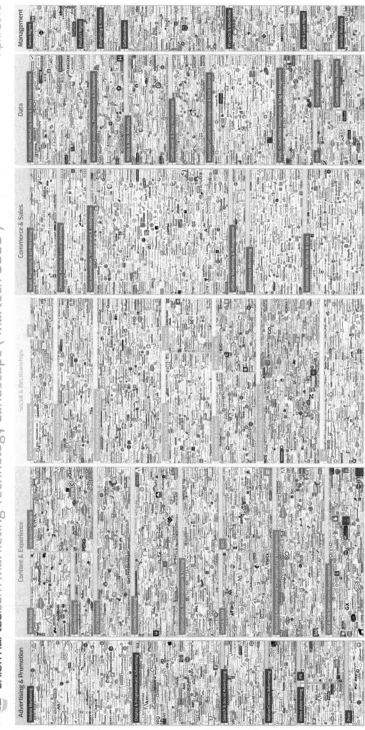

Copyright © 2018 Marketing Technology Media LLC (See http://chiefmartec.com/2018/04/marketing-technology-landscape-supergraphic-2018/ for details and sources.

Produced by Scott Brinker (@chiefmartec), Anand Thaker (@AnandThaker), and Blair Green Brands.

FIGURE 7.1 The MarTech landscape
Source: Created by Scott Brinker. Used with permission.

some marketing processes. It can be detailed or visionary, a schematic or an infographic; the format doesn't matter as much as the usefulness of the content in helping to communicate and advance the impact that a technology investment has on capabilities and performance.

Blueprints like this can help marketing executives make smarter decisions for both new and incremental investments by painting a clearer picture of which marketing and ad technologies have already been adopted, the ways they connect with each other (or don't), and how they connect customers and prospects to internal resources and processes. As a result, it helps communicate a vision, with different internal audiences, in a way that nontechnical C-level leaders can digest—and importantly, it can help marketers more easily and effectively sell that vision to key stakeholders. It also can help make the case for increased investment and serve as a guide for identifying holes or areas of weakness. See the following list for the anatomy of a successful MarTech Blueprint.

The Anatomy of a Successful MarTech Blueprint

It answers these questions:

1. What's our vision for the customer experience and journey?
2. What's the desired state of marketing technology to guide the buyer journey?
3. What pieces do we have in place, and what's left to add?
4. Are we using what we have—scope, scale, geography, enablement?
5. Have we integrated what we have?
6. Are there duplications or unnecessary capabilities?
7. How can we align our technology road map with data flow, marketing capabilities, and customer experiences?

One of the most significant benefits of the MarTech Blueprint is that it creates a single view of how technology integrates across the entire enterprise. This visualization—which should be updated regularly—does not just constitute a valuable auditing and decision-making tool. It also can enhance communication among all stakeholders, including board members and C-suite executives, other departments and business units, all members of the marketing department, and current and prospective technology providers.

Who Uses a MarTech Blueprint

MarTech Blueprints (see figure 7.2 and the examples in the appendix at the end of this chapter) are developed and used by CMOs, marketing executives, marketing operations professionals, information technology (IT) teams, marketing systems integrators, and others to visualize the current marketing architecture, the ways in which the systems and tools connect, the processes they support, and how they affect customer experience and the value of marketing to the business. Most importantly, they help marketers identify which MarTech solutions are needed to help deliver on the strategic marketing plan.

For example, consider figure 7.2. This MarTech Blueprint defines the solutions that are the most important areas to address according to the marketing and technology teams. Each of the boxes represents a different type of technology, allowing the team to use this structure to determine whether they currently have all the solutions outlined on the blueprint. Who develops and then analyzes and interprets the MarTech Blueprint? Often, a steering team of key cross-functional representatives, such as IT, marketing, and finance, can lead the development and analysis of the MarTech Blueprint.

Here are the steps that teams can take to develop and use the MarTech Blueprint:

Step 1: Identify the business (marketing) goals from the strategic marketing plan. These will be a compass and will ultimately determine the priorities as teams explore enabling new or

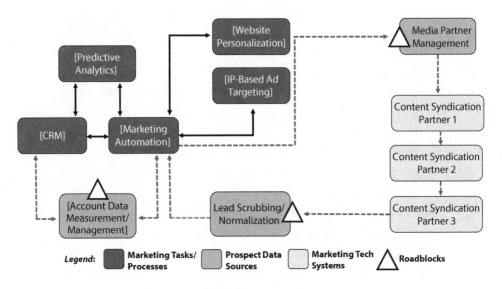

FIGURE 7.2 A simple example of a MarTech Blueprint

improved capabilities in their marketing efforts. Teams must also be clear about how the identified project or initiative syncs with the BES and the strategic marketing plan.

Step 2: Define the available resources. Because human and financial resources are not infinite, choices will always have to be made to ensure successful execution. This effort includes (1) identifying the roles and skill sets needed; (2) assessing gaps in the available skills versus the needed skills (and then determining how to fill the gaps, either through outsourced solutions or hiring additional talent); (3) identifying the amount of time that teams have to spend on the initiative; and (4) determining the budget (both the ideal and the maximum amount for the project).

Step 3: Take inventory of technology. It's important to take inventory of the existing technology and systems, documenting the interconnectedness via a visual diagram; this helps ensure that the team understands how the current technologies fit together (or don't) and where they connect (e.g., consumer-facing experiences or employee workstations). This effort is critical for three reasons: (1) for seeing if there is a way to use existing technology to address the business need instead of investing in more tech; (2) for understanding how any potential new technology will (or will not) integrate with the tech that is already being used; and (3) for providing a baseline understanding of the technology landscape that enables a before-and-after visualization, helping to communicate a vision and plan to non-tech people.

Step 4: Take inventory of marketing processes. Once technology systems are documented, the next step is to capture and document the current marketing processes in relation to technology. What steps or processes should be taken to analyze customer data and execute various marketing (e.g., email campaigns, ad campaigns, lead-generation programs, and/or web or in-store checkout processes)? The goal here is to find the processes that can be optimized or automated to help marketers focus on the strategic, high-impact initiatives.

Step 5: Create the MarTech Blueprint. The next step is to put it all together and develop the MarTech Blueprint in a visual diagram. This can be done via a document, a Microsoft PowerPoint slide, or even something less formal, such as a photo of a whiteboard diagram. The important point is to have something to discuss and share with others.

Step 6: Analyze the MarTech Blueprint. With the full view now visualized, teams can get to work analyzing the MarTech Blueprint. What to look for here is what needs to be added, changed, or eliminated to enable the new marketing/business capability or initiative that has been identified. This analysis is looking for the technology-process requirements (what really needs to be done), gaps (missing tech or processes), bottlenecks (manual efforts that can be automated or systems that can be fully integrated), and/or areas of redundancy (cost or time savings) that need to be addressed to enable the new capability or fix a problem.

Step 7: Merchandise (i.e., share) the results. One of the most powerful benefits of the MarTech Blueprint is a "single view of the truth" that can be shared and leveraged to create meaningful discussions within the team, with stakeholders, and with current and prospective tech providers. This can be shared in planning sessions, during staff meetings, and when purchase decisions are being evaluated.

Step 8: Use and modify the Blueprint. Once teams have the MarTech Blueprint, they can use and adapt it for all Mar-Tech-related projects and initiatives. This ability to see the whole picture enables the key players to be in sync and more informed regarding decisions, including prioritizing investments when marketing goals shift with business requirements.

The MarTech Blueprint: A Case Study

The following is a case study[6] of how a CMO for a global firm was able to use the MarTech Blueprint to align the entire enterprise on a vision of how to use technology to enable a better consumer experience. The firm in this case is a multibillion-dollar organization providing software and IT applications to some of the world's most innovative companies. The marketing team has regularly been recognized for its innovative and modern approach to marketing, including the skillful use of technology to improve results. See figure 7.3 for an example of the final MarTech Blueprint.

The marketing operations and analytics teams organized an effort to develop and activate the MarTech Blueprint. Their objectives were (1) to better identify, manage, and prioritize tech investments and initiatives and (2) to improve the customer experience and journey to deliver superior business results. The specific business results that

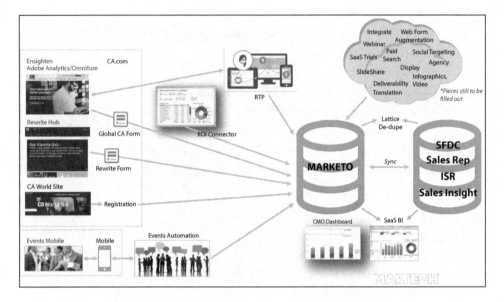

FIGURE 7.3 A completed MarTech Blueprint

needed to be improved were lead generation and customer acquisition. Inbound marketing initiatives (which were a major source of MarTech investment) had hit a ceiling in terms of the quantity and quality of leads being generated. The team needed to efficiently scale outbound demand generation (i.e., paid media) efforts to pump new prospective customers into the sales pipeline.

After identifying the budget assigned to the project and developing a map of the original technology system (i.e., a visual representation of the technology system across the enterprise), the team met to identify the specific challenges associated with achieving their objectives. There were three primary challenges: (1) out-of-sync budget-pacing issues and disconnected manual lead-management processes; (2) inefficient methods of identifying, testing, and onboarding new lead sources; and (3) inaccurate lead-generation decisions that were based on gut feelings rather than data.

The team then began to develop a MarTech Blueprint designed to achieve the objectives outlined and address the challenges identified. Specifically, the team did the following:

1. The team evaluated the existing technology system and solutions to see if there was a way to improve lead-generation efforts. It was essential that any additional technology or process could seamlessly integrate with the team's original inbound marketing efforts; this meant that any new or improved systems designed to identify and generate new leads would have to flow into the database and marketing automation systems that were currently in place.

2. After evaluating the original systems, the team members discovered that they needed to identify a new solution, as their current systems would not accomplish what the team needed. Therefore, they developed a MarTech Blueprint. Because of the criticality of this initiative, this discovery meant an investment in and prioritization of this project over others.

3. The team shared their MarTech Blueprint with a handful of potential vendors (and internal stakeholders) to serve as a specific scope of work for what was needed. The process to identify the ultimate solutions provider with whom to partner took sixty to ninety days.

4. The MarTech Blueprint framework was used within the marketing department to understand where technology and processes could help create a more efficient way to use all lead sources to scale marketing efforts. The MarTech Blueprint was also used across the organization to help explain why the MarTech investment was needed and how it would work. Essentially, it served as a training tool to educate all stakeholders on the new process and show how it connected with existing process and data flows. The MarTech Blueprint–driven process also helped

identify a better way to organize the demand-generation and marketing-operations roles required to execute the department's lead-generation and customer-acquisition programs.

5. Because this outbound lead-generation effort was laid out within the overall marketing framework and easily understood via the MarTech Blueprint, it was an effective way to align C-suite leaders and board members with the project, budget, and plan.

Because the team was comfortable with the MarTech Blueprint, the entire process went quickly. They were able to identify the objectives, identify a solution, choose a solutions provider, and integrate the firm's systems and processes. The business results included (1) an increase of 36 percent in outbound leads generated, (2) a 59.2 percent decrease in effective cost per lead, (3) a 23 percent increase in lead conversion, and (4) forty hours saved each month by shifting from manual to automated lead data processing.

Summary

Modern marketing organizations are using technology to enable new capabilities to keep pace with the changing expectations of their customers and to deliver better results from their marketing investments. Like the many other business functions that have been automated using technology (e.g., manufacturing, human resources, IT, and sales), marketing has become powered by technology. The shift to digital and data-driven marketing will only continue to fuel the use of technology by marketers in the future. The key to success is to create a vision and lead the organization in a specific direction, and the MarTech Blueprint is an important tool that can help brand strategists efficiently and effectively allocate resources to smart tech investments that yield results in both the short and long term.

Appendix

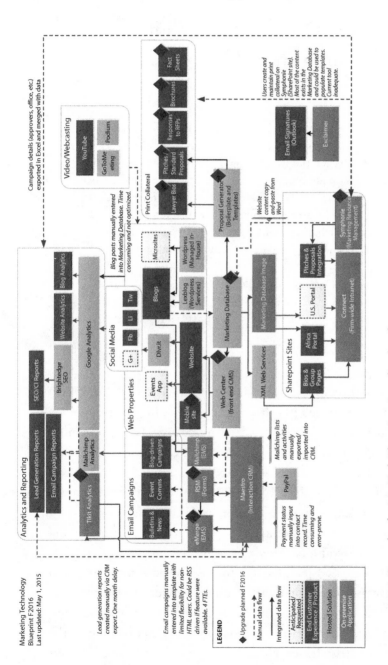

FIGURE AP 7.1 Example of a MarTech Blueprint: Canadian law firm

Source: Brinker, Scott (2015). "Marketing Technology Blueprint F2016," *ChiefMartec.com*, [available at: http://cdn.chiefmartec. com/wpcontent/uploads/2015/06/canadianlawfirm_marketing_tech_stack.png]. Used with permission. For other examples, see Brinker, Scott, "Datapipe Marketing Stack & Data Flow," http://cdn.chiefmartec.com/wp-content/uploads/2015/06/data-pipe_marketing_tech_stack.png, Scott Brinker, "IntelligenceBank, http://cdn.chiefmartec.com/wp-content/uploads/2015/06 /intelligencebank_marketing_tech_stack.jpg, and Scott Brinker, "*Bloomreach Marketing Technology as of June 2015*," http:// chiefmartec.com/2015/06/21-marketing-technology-stacks-shared-stackies-awards/.

8

Key Opinion Leader and Influencer Mapping

Influencers are the key to the digital marketplace. . . . According to recent studies, user-generated content accounts for at least 25 percent of search results for the world's top 20 brands. Meanwhile, sites such as Facebook are promoting authentic user-generated content to create and nurture personal connections on their platform. Leveraging an influencer for your content marketing efforts can enhance your search engine rankings in a shorter amount of time.

—MAHER JABER, CEO AND COFOUNDER, BRANDFIT[1]

We truly believe in the power of influencer marketing. We use it to connect our work with people—to reach out and to engage people.

—LUIS DI COMO, EXECUTIVE VICE PRESIDENT, UNILEVER[2]

CHAPTER 7 INTRODUCED the Marketing Technology (MarTech) Blueprint, a tool designed to help combine marketing and technology to enhance the consumer experience. In this chapter, I delve into influencer mapping, which is commonly referred to as *key opinion leader (KOL) marketing* in Asia and in other places around the world, to introduce a tool that enables marketers to ensure that their resource investment will deliver on their strategic marketing plan.

Before we dive into developing a map for an influencer marketing program, let's look at an example of influencer marketing. In 2015, Emirates Airlines used Jennifer Aniston in a television ad campaign to help drive awareness of their premium service experience. The spots were considered successful, as they generated a suitable number of YouTube views. However, in late 2015, Emirates gave the popular techpreneur Casey Neistat an early membership in their premier class of service. Why? They were hoping that Neistat, as a significant influencer among Emirates Airlines' target consumers, would share his experience with his followers on various social media sites. It worked. Neistat created videos raving about the new Emirates service. The two videos received over 63 million views and the attention helped Emirates earn praise in *Maxim* and *GQ*, among others.

This example of a celebrity endorser (Aniston) used in conjunction with an influencer (Neistat) shows that while both can have profound influence over their audiences through social media, the knowledge, skill, and advice that emanate from an influencer is often valued more, as it is connected with a source of expertise. While Tiger Woods, a professional golfer, has endorsed everything from cars to watches to consulting firms to razors, powerful influencers tend to "stay in their lane," talking only about things about which they have expertise.

What Is Influencer Marketing?

Before the tech boom, marketers used various channels—such as newspapers, magazines, billboards, and television advertisements—to communicate with consumers to shape their beliefs and behaviors. While direct communication from company to consumer was pervasive, marketers knew that word-of-mouth marketing (WOMM), or the sharing of stories and referrals from one consumer to another, has in many ways been a more trusted—and therefore more effective—method of influencing consumers. A 1980s television commercial for Faberge Organics (a hair-care product) captured this effect by suggesting that a satisfied customer told two friends, who told two friends, and so on, and so on, and so on . . .

Despite the power of WOMM, it has been historically difficult to influence, manage, or measure. Consequently, it often ended up being a positive side effect of good product experiences rather than a strategic objective that marketers proactively managed. However, the advent of technology-enabled social media has unlocked the potential for marketers to use WOMM as an important part of their marketing plans. Today, marketers have a greater ability to identify, engage, track, and measure the influencers who shape consumers' beliefs and behavior through social sharing (e.g., Twitter, Pinterest, Facebook, WeChat, Weibo, etc.).

Countries such as China arguably lead the world in developing sophisticated KOL programs that drive awareness, brand perception, affinity, loyalty, and sales. Steven Chang, a former executive at Tencent, the parent company of WeChat, one of the world's most popular social sharing apps with nearly a billion monthly users, suggests: "While many firms focus on buying media, Chinese companies have been for years focused on creating engaging, storytelling, and belief-changing programs through KOLs. Most Chinese marketers now think about influencers first, as they are often faster, more efficient, and more effective than other marketing methods."[3] What follows are three case studies on influencer marketing programs and a tool to help connect your program to your business objectives and strategies.

The Tencent Case

In 2017, Tencent developed a campaign called "Next Idea." It was a contest aimed at China's youth, designed to identify the next big innovation ideas. To drive immediate awareness, Tencent used KOLs as the centerpiece of their strategy, partnering with two well-known individuals to drive virality and interest. The first was Karry Wang, an eighteen-year-old pop singer, and the second was the noted physicist Stephen Hawking. This combination of a leading Chinese business partnering with a young, popular singer and arguably the best-known contemporary physicist may be unusual, but the unlikely pairing drove interest. On the morning of November 24, 2017, Wang asked

Hawking a question about the future of humanity in a prerecorded video, which was shared on Weibo (China's version of Twitter). In the afternoon of that same day, Hawking replied via another prerecorded video. By the end of the day, this exchange became the number-one-trending topic, with nearly 30 million views, 2 million shares, 49,000 comments, and more than 500,000 likes. Tencent's Next Idea following increased from 20 to over 52,000 in one day. Imagine the cost of creating these two short videos compared to a traditional advertising program. Now imagine how long it would take to drive awareness using traditional advertising techniques versus what Tencent achieved in a twenty-four-hour period.

The Volkswagen Touareg Case

On Touareg's fifteenth anniversary in 2017, Volkswagen faced a problem.[4] How should the company market this niche, yet legendary sport utility vehicle (SUV) to as many of the target consumer group as possible? How could they quickly reach out and expand the fan base? Volkswagen knew that they needed something groundbreaking to break through the clutter. In cooperation with Tencent, Volkswagen invited a series of high-profile KOLs with different backgrounds to travel for six months to retrace the route of the legendary Silk Road, visiting famous cities along the way. Each trek was filmed, resulting in eighteen episodes that were brought to life by a retelling of historical and cultural tales, mixed with personal tales of happiness and hardship from the celebrities themselves.

The series was a significant success on many dimensions. At more than 9,000 kilometers across two continents, it was the longest recorded SUV journey in history. The locations and stories featured on the show were all directly intertwined with the DNA of the Touareg brand. Combining beautiful cinematography with entertaining storytelling and personally interesting tidbits from the KOLS with a celebration of the Touareg's fifteenth anniversary had an impact beyond each three-minute episode. It was the very first native KOL programming in the form of entertainment to be aired on Tencent News (one of the largest news platforms in China).

The Procter and Gamble SK-II Case Study

As an example of a unique way of thinking about influencers, Aaron Shapiro, founder and chief executive officer (CEO) of Huge (a digital marketing firm with operations throughout Asia, North and South America, and Europe, serving over 300 companies, including 25 percent of the *Fortune* 50), provided a case of how his firm worked with SK-II, a Japanese cosmetics brand owned by Procter & Gamble (P&G), to create some business-affecting KOL programs in China: "We developed a campaign that featured a well-known influencer in China (actresses Jiang Xin and Tang Wei) . . . they were developing a lot of content about SK-II—and we helped by providing information about the brand." They produced a short film called *Life Has No Limit*, that went viral over Chinese social media. The film details a Chinese cultural phenomenon referred to as "leftover women," which fights dated social norms and promotes female independence to create and pursue their own dreams. The actresses shared the video with their followers, and the brand saw a measurable lift in business results. The video received 17 million views in just two days on Miaopai, a Chinese video-sharing and livestreaming service. During the first week of the campaign, eighty-six influencers mentioned SK-II in 100 posts, generating social media value in excess of 15 million Chinese yuans. It was also named one of the Top 8 Influencer programs in China in 2017.

While this is a common way of leveraging influencers, Shapiro indicated that this wasn't a minor, tertiary priority. Instead, the KOL program, of which this is just one example, was a key cornerstone of Huge's marketing. While many companies may dabble with influencer marketing, assigning it to junior managers and giving it little financial or managerial support, this KOL program was going to drive success (or failure), so it was assigned both talented marketers and sufficient financial resources.

To demonstrate how far SK-II has developed the KOL program, Shapiro shared an example of what the brand did in China on Singles' Day (November 11, 2016). SK-II created a virtual reality experience and shared it with the influencers of influencers. It was designed to affect a few individuals, who would in turn affect the key target influencers. To illustrate how this works, assume that there is a group of women with significant social influence regarding fashion, and the goal was to affect their thinking. Rather than partnering with these influencers directly, Shapiro's team partnered with the key individuals who influence the female bloggers. This type of program would be relatively groundbreaking in the United States.

The Power of Influencer Marketing

The potential of influencer marketing is undeniable. One study indicates that the return on investment (ROI) is roughly eleven times that of other traditional forms of digital media. Among teens, YouTube stars are seventeen times more engaging than mainstream stars, and 74 percent of consumers say that they turn to social networks for guidance on purchase decisions. There are three key reasons why influencer marketing is a powerful complement to many traditional marketing programs:

1. **It can create reach efficiently.** In the Tencent example, the brand was able to garner over 30 million views. What is the traditional or digital media cost to reach 30 million customers in less than a twenty-four-hour period?
2. **It can drive awareness quickly.** Because of the nature of social media itoften drives awareness faster than traditional methods such as television advertising, which require repetition

over time. In the Tencent case, on the day that the videos were shared, the topic became the number-one-trending topic on Weibo and the videos had nearly 30 million views. This happened within hours—not days or months—of the first video airing. Traditional awareness-generating methods take much longer. In interviews I conducted with C-level leaders in China (including Chinese-based and multinational companies), the multinationals generally felt that China has a speed advantage. One of the reasons is the country's superior ability to create content that engages the target through influencer marketing programs.

3. **It is often more trusted.** Messages that come from firms are obviously promoting their products and services. Consequently, there is bias in these messages, as they are created to put companies in the best possible light. Consumers generally understand this. However, messages from knowledgable, trusted, relatable, and respected sources transmitted through social media can carry greater weight. There is an expectation that when these individuals promote a product, it is an honest and trusted reflection of their beliefs because the influencers are putting their own reputations at risk when they endorse a product. And this is an important distinction. There is a fine line between being a shill for a company and promoting something that you honestly and objectively believe in. In the SK-II example, the actresses strongly supported the central message, and it is unclear whether they were paid. The same goes for the Tencent case, which used recorded messages from Stephen Hawking to promote innovation in China. Influencer marketing is powerful, in part, because it is often perceived to be more objective than and divorced from paid celebrity endorsements.

Luis Di Como, executive vice president at Unilever, indicates that the company uses influencer marketing not only to reach out and engage people, but also to "build trust and credibility for our brands and to bring a really great brand experience to the people that we serve. . . . We are using influencer marketing for Dove across the whole spectrum. In some cases, we use influencers to talk about the features and benefits of the products. . . . But more and more, we are using them to talk about the idea to buy into—to talk about the brand value, of why the brand exists, and the purpose of the brand."[5]

In the end, the power of this kind of marketing lies in the fact that the comments are coming from trusted individuals who are perceived to have expertise and objectivity about the product or service and who have a large and engaged social following.

The Next Step: Engaging Microinfluencers

Shapiro's example—targeting the influencers of influencers—is also known as *microinfluencer marketing*. Although they typically have smaller social networks, microinfluencers can offer strong engagement at a significantly lower cost than the biggest social media stars. For this reason, companies like Unilever have developed strategies to identify those individuals who influence the more difficult-to-access and often more expensive influencers. As an example of microinfluencers, Leadtail, a social media insights research company, creates an annual report that identifies the top influencers of chief marketing officers (CMOs). These individuals, such as Tamara McCleary, Marsha Collier, Margaret Molloy, and Scott Brinker, are followed and read by a high number of CMOs. As opposed to just cold calling and attempting to set up a meeting with these CMOs, marketers can save time and money by using McCleary, Molloy, or Brinker to write or tweet about a company and how a particular firm can help CMOs.

In Shapiro's case, the brand's objectives (as outlined in its strategic marketing plan) required driving the highest level of awareness, at minimal investment, and as fast as possible. With this set of objectives, a key strategy included developing an influencer program, in which leveraging microinfluencers was one tactic.

A Prerequisite to Developing an Influencer Marketing Program

Before implementing an influencer marketing program, it is crucial to understand the strategic business plan and whether influencer marketing is related to a key strategy that will help achieve specific business goals. If influencer marketing maps onto the strategic plans for the business, then continue developing the plan. If it doesn't flow from the business objectives and strategies, then it shouldn't be adopted.

This is one of the important reasons why marketers must develop strategic plans and ensure that their tactical choices will achieve the desired business objectives. In meeting after meeting, you will be presented with new, different, and exciting tactical opportunities. I have watched marketers crumble under the weight of tactics piled upon more tactics. The strategic marketing plan can be amended, but it first helps the marketer thoughtfully and rigorously develop the set of activities most likely to drive success and then, once developed, enables the marketer to pull it out and use it to remind the organization of what is and isn't in the plan. If it makes sense to add an influencer marketing program, then the strategic marketing plan can be used as a basis for labor and project management.

Influencer Marketing Mapping: A Template

While the discussion in this chapter illustrates how influencer mapping is developed and used, I share a template for an influencer marketing map in table 8.1. Although there are many methods of mapping, and each should be customized for the specific business context and conditions, this can serve as a starting point to help provide a structured approach to thinking about influencer marketing.

TABLE 8.1

Influencer marketing map

Strategic Alignment		Action Plans		Measurement
Business Objectives and Goals	**Brand Message**	**"Who"**	**"What"**	**Track and Measure**
What are the business objectives and goals—in words and in numbers—that this program must deliver on? What is the specific strategy and/or tactic that the influencer marketing program supports? Essentially, what is the business imperative that makes developing an influencer marketing program critical?	Who is the target consumer? What elements of the brand essence statement (BES) is the influencer marketing program designed to support, strengthen, or solidify?	Who is/are the influencer(s)? What is the rationale for how they support the objectives, strategy, target, and BES?	Given the "Who" and "Where," what is the plan to activate the influencer marketing program? Essentially, what is the idea behind the execution?	What are the specific number based goals that the program needs to hit to be successful? Be specific and include the numbers and when this should occur (e.g., day 1, month 1, etc.). What is the measurement tracker that you plan to use (e.g., a dashboard, a report, etc.)?
		"Where"	**"When"**	
		Which channels are most effective to reach the target consumer (i.e., Twitter, Facebook, LinkedIn, WeChat, Pinterest, etc.)? What is the priority?	When is the plan to be executed? Day, time, etc.?	

Influencer Marketing Mapping: An Example Using the Tencent "Next Idea" Case Study

Figure 8.1 shows an example of the influencer marketing mapping process, from strategy to action plans to measurement.

In the "Next Idea" scenario, Tencent had a business objective to drive significant awareness of the program as quickly and efficiently as possible. The short-term measure of success was the degree of awareness

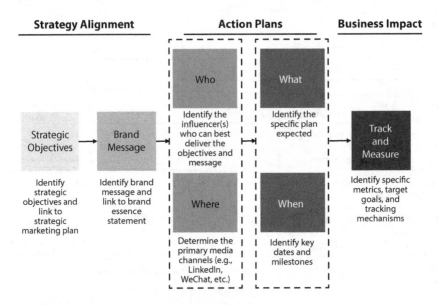

FIGURE 8.1 The process of influencer marketing mapping

created among the target population within a very rapidperiod of time (i.e., a week). The long-term measure of success was the number of young people who submitted ideas. Because time was a critical element of the business objectives, a key strategy was to adopt KOL/influencer marketing to drive awareness. In this case, influencer marketing was a central strategy, critical to achieving the business objective and success measures.

The second step is to understand the link to the BES. In many cases, this is a time where influencer marketing can go awry. If influencer marketing is central to achieving business objectives, it has to be done within the confines of the BES or the guardrails that ensure that all actions are communicating the brand strategy. At this point, you want to define the target and the elements of the BES that the influencer marketing program is designed to affect:

With Next Idea, the connection to Tencent's BES was straight-forward—to help establish the company as a leading innovator in

China—a firm that not only is innovative, but supports the development of innovation among China's youth. This effort was connected not only to the benefit of Tencent (a leading innovator), but also to the values of the company (to support and promote innovation in China).

The third step is to develop the action plans. Because this mapping process is designed to peg off of the business objectives and brand strategy, the goal is to think broadly about possibilities. Anchoring your influencer marketing program on objectives and strategies, as opposed to a specific influencer, is crucial to ensure that you aren't wasting resources. However, it is equally important to brainstorm a number of possible influencer marketing partners (i.e., "who") before deciding on a specific path. In concert with "who" is "where," "what," and "when." In other words, which communication channels are most relevant for the target, and therefore should be prioritized? What is the specific plan? When are the key milestones? The who and the where are often determined first and help determine the what and the when:

In Next Idea, "who" was arguably the most difficult step. The company wanted to identify somebody relevant to the target and somebody who was an expert in innovation and science, ideally a single person who could achieve both objectives. After deciding it would be difficult to find one person, the firm identified two influencers—one who was very relevant to the target (Chinese youth) and was known to be interested in science and one who was an expert in science (i.e., Stephen Hawking). The "where" was simple—the marketers wanted to focus on the company's own social media channels—and the "what" flowed directly from the decision to have two influencers. Because there were two influencers, the decision was made to create a dialogue between the two in a question-and-answer format. Finally, the "when" decision was based on when the firm believed that it could generate high levels of engagement with the target and would work given the project milestones.

The final step is to track and measure the progress of the project. What are the measures that will determine success? How do these connect to the strategic marketing plan? What vehicles will you use to track the measures, and with what frequency (i.e., hourly, daily, weekly, monthly)? These decisions are critical to map out before implementation begins in order to ensure that you know how you will determine whether the program was successful:

With Next Idea, Tencent had two sets of milestones: (1) short-term awareness-building goals, and (2) long-term idea submissions. Because of the desire to drive immediate awareness, the firm tracked progress hourly for the first week and then moved to weekly. The long-term measurement was simple. Tencent was able to track the number of Chinese kids that submitted innovation ideas for the contest. On both sets of criteria, the marketing team had specific goals. The results exceeded the goals, so the program was determined to be a success.

Summary

Influencer marketing is growing in its relevance and use across the globe. Its value in creating trusted awareness faster and often cheaper than traditional marketing methods makes it especially appealing. The central challenge is to develop programs in a way that supports both the business's strategic priorities and the brand's reputation and image. And this is not necessarily easy to do. The influencer marketing map is a tool that can enable you to ensure that your influencer marketing effort is directly connected to and is a consequence of your business objectives and brand message. In chapter 9, we will finish the marketing planning section of the book by considering the different ways in which brands can be measured.

9

Brand Measurement Methods

> Brands—whether product, service, retail or corporate, consumer or business-to-business—are demonstrably the most important and sustainable asset any organization has.
>
> —RITA CLIFTON[1]

BEING A CAPABLE MARKETING strategist means being able to measure the outcome of actions and programs. Thus far, we have focused on the development of strategies and plans that can help marketers effectively create and manage growth brands. While creating growth brands is a common goal across firms, a key challenge that marketers face is the measurement of a brand. As Peter Drucker has said, "The purpose of a business is to create a customer."[2] The conduit through which a customer is created is the brand, and as such, developing strong brands is a priority across most firms and industries. As an example of the importance of brands, consider the following perspective provided by Fidelity, an investment firm, to investors on the consumer discretionary industry:

> Strong brand allegiance can protect companies against the substitution of their products with cheaper alternatives. Further, companies that can control the distribution and pricing of their goods are better equipped to maintain strong sales margins. For example, certain manufacturers of innovative sneakers, . . . women's lingerie,

and specialty coffee continue to grow in popularity with consumers. These brands have strong customer connections and tend to distribute their products through their own stores, and thus are able to maintain full pricing. My view is that these types of companies offer the potential for the best sales and earnings growth potential. . . . Conversely, companies that widely distribute easily substituted, commoditized products through internet retailers and big-box stores are likely to face challenges.[3]

What does it mean to measure a brand? Is it about the worth of the brand? Is it about the target consumer's perception, or is it about how well known the brand is? The purpose of this final chapter regarding marketing tools is to (1) provide a conceptual model that frames the ways in which brands can be measured, (2) describe the key measurement methods, and (3) provide commonly used examples for each measurement method. While chapter 7 provided a tool to integrate marketing and technology, and chapter 8 introduced influencer mapping, a new tool to synchronize influencer marketing with the strategic marketing plan, this chapter offers a way of thinking about how to measure brands to create greater accountability.

Why Measure Brands?

In general, CEOs would like to see greater accountability from their marketers. In research conducted by the Fournaise Group, most of them believe that "marketers can't prove that they drive growth."[4] It is up to marketers to lead the efforts to measure performance, strategic plans, and the overall brand. By measuring brands, marketers and firm leaders are able to (1) guide marketing strategy and tactical decisions, (2) assess in-market progress against a desired positioning strategy, (3) assess the extendibility of a brand, (4) evaluate the effectiveness of marketing decisions, (5) track the brand's strength compared with that of competitors, and (6) assign a financial value to the brand.

The benefit of measuring brand health and performance is clear. The challenge is in identifying and understanding the various tools that can be used to measure brands and then choosing the right one for the right purpose.

Four Areas of Brand Measurement

Because of the myriad methods used to measure brands, CEOs, chief marketing officers (CMOs), and chief financial officers (CFOs) may approach measurement differently, compounding the difficulty of gaining an aligned perspective on the health, strength, and value of a brand.

Figure 9.1 outlines a model of four areas of brand-health measurement. Part of the challenge in measuring brands is determining which perspective to base the measurement on—the consumer's or the firm's. This matters because measuring a brand from the consumer's perspective means understanding the consumer's perception of the brand. In contrast, measuring the strength of a brand from the firm's perspective may include measuring the financial value of the brand.

In figure 9.1, the two perspectives are integrated because firm-level outcomes such as revenue, volume, and profit growth (i.e., financial metrics) are the result of consumer-level effects such as brand

Consumer Knowledge	**Consumer Perception**	**Consumer Behavior**	**Financial Valuation**
Brand Knowledge • Awareness • Familiarity • Degree of understanding	Brand Image • Overall feeling/ perception and associations Brand Attributes • Perceptions of brand attributes (disaggregated brand understanding) • Product related • Not product–related	Consumer Behavior • Loyalty (customer lifetime value • Price premium • Likelihood to recommend (Net Promoter Score)	Financial Valuation • Branded earnings • Future earnings potential • Royalty rate • Price premium

FIGURE 9.1 A sample model of brand measurement

knowledge, brand image, and consumer behavior.[5] This model integrates the various aspects of brand measurement into one framework to help marketers lead others in the firm to understand the many ways to measure brand health. Importantly, this model can also be useful in helping marketers understand which method may be most appropriate based on a particular business objective.[6]

Knowledge Metrics

One dimension of brand health is the degree to which the consumer is aware of, familiar with, and knowledgeable about the brand. Awareness and a degree of familiarity with a brand are required before consumers can have a perception about the brand. While measuring awareness and familiarity may seem simple, there are critical questions that need to be asked prior to measurement. For example, who should be measured (e.g., the users of the brand, anybody within the target group, the general population, and so forth)? How is familiarity defined and measured? Awareness and familiarity are often measured using a number of different perspectives, such as (1) awareness among the general population and among the target group, and (2) degree of familiarity among the target group, brand users, and competitors' customers.

Perception Metrics

Once consumers obtain a degree of brand familiarity, they are able to form an impression about the brand. This impression can be at an aggregate level (e.g., an overall brand impression) or on a more specific level (e.g., an individual brand-attribute impression). One of the most popular dimensions of brand health that sophisticated marketing companies regularly measure centers on a brand's overall image and individual attributes. The overall brand image is typically measured by asking a general question such as, "Overall, how would you rate Amazon?" In contrast, individual brand attributes are a dis-aggregated view of the brand. For example, Amazon could measure several aspects of the brand, including (1) functional attributes (e.g., navigation ease, choice ease, checkout ease, checkout speed, value, quality of products, and price of products); (2) experiential attributes (e.g., the joy or fun of the shopping experience); and even (3) personal attributes (e.g., is a brand I admire, is a reliable brand, is a fun brand).

A primary goal of marketers is to improve ownership of key attri-butes that represent the brand's positioning strategy, which is why it is so important to disaggregate a brand and understand its underlying strengths and weaknesses. For example, assume that the positioning of Dyson (which sells vacuum cleaners, hair dryers, air treatment devices, and heaters) is to deliver better electrical appliances through superior engineering and contemporary design. Over time, through product inno-vation, brand actions, and marketing communication, Dyson market-ers will attempt to generate a superior image relative to competitors on attributes such as, "is an innovative brand," "makes products that are contemporary," and "makes better-designed products." These individual attributes, as well as overall measures of the brand, will be used to assess how well the company is delivering on the desired positioning. When there is a gap between the stated brand positioning and reality, this pro-vides insight into the specific area or areas that marketing and the firm in general need to address. For example, if Dyson desired to own "superior innovation," but research indicated that in the minds of consumers, the brand didn't have a statistically significant better rating on this attribute relative to a key competitor, that would help the brand team know that its actions (e.g., design, technical innovation, communications, etc.) were not delivering on the desired perception. The team could then seek to understand the reason behind the gap and develop a plan to address it.

Consequently, once a brand positioning strategy is determined, a critical way to assess the brand's in-market progress on that position-ing is to measure performance on the desired attributes versus key competitors. As an example, Walmart's positioning is centered on "superior value—lowest prices." In measurement on brand attributes such as "superior value" and "lowest prices," you would expect to see that if Walmart has effectively achieved its desired positioning, the firm owns these attributes relative to all other competitors.

Consumer Behavior Metrics

Once consumers obtain a degree of brand familiarity that develops into a perception of the brand, they behave in a way that is based on that perspective. They can purchase a product (or not), become loyal to a product (or not), or recommend a product to a friend (or not). Consumer behavior can take a variety of forms. For example, as the Fidelity quote that started this chapter suggests, consumers are typically willing to pay more for a product with a more favorable brand image. Other measures include the degree to which consumers try a product, repurchase a product, become loyal to a product, and are willing to recommend that product to others. All these measures are associated with actions that consumers take as a consequence of knowledge of and perception about the brand.

Financial Metrics

The final dimension of brand health is the outcome that occurs from consumer familiarity with a brand, the consumer's perception of a brand, and ultimately the consumer's behavior—that is, the financial metrics. One of the most important elements when addressing CEO concerns is tying marketing actions to brand health measures *and* financial outcomes. The concept of brand valuation has broadened considerably since 1988, when Interbrand, a branding consultancy, pioneered a method that is now used in many marketing strategy and financial decisions.[7]

Trying to value a brand or determine the degree to which the brand contributes to firm performance is difficult. Despite the challenge, one method is to determine the pricing power that a branded product has over a generic one. For example, what is a consumer willing to pay for a generic bottle of soda versus one with a Coca-Cola label on it? The incremental price that the consumer is willing to pay is a tangible, financial measure of brand value. Another measure of brand value can be a royalty rate that a firm is willing to pay to use the brand name. Luxury brands such as Nicole Miller and Vera Wang often license their brand names. The amount they receive in the form of a licensing fee is a clear measure of brand value. Finally, when a firm is sold to another firm, there must be a dollar value assigned to the brand by law. There are accounting and financial standards that guide firms in determining brand value in these circumstances.

Commonly Used Methods to Measure Brand Health

While there are numerous ways to assess knowledge, image, behavior, and financial metrics, in the appendix at the end of the chapter, I have included several commonly used methods. Table 9.1 summarizes which

TABLE 9.1

Commonly used methods to measure brand health

Index	Consumer knowledge	Consumer perception	Consumer behavior	Financial valuation
Millward Brown's BrandZ		X	X	X
Interbrand		X		X
Brand Finance		X	X	X
Y&R BrandAsset Valuator	X	X		
Net Promoter Score			X	
Customer-Based Brand Equity Model		X		
Harris Poll EquiTrend	X	X		
Harris Poll Reputation Quotient		X		
Brand Equity Monitor	X	X		
Brand Attachment Model for Digital Interactions		X	X	

dimension of brand health each tool assesses. For example, Millward Brown's BrandZ measurement method incorporates elements of perception, behavior, and financial metrics. As the table illustrates, most commonly used methods designed to measure brands tend to be centered on understanding the consumer's perception of the brand, with fewer methods designed to measure the financial value of brands.

Appendix

Ten Methods of Brand Assessment

Millward Brown's BrandZ

Objective: Millward Brown's BrandZ index "combines extensive and ongoing consumer research with rigorous financial analysis"[8] and is used by publications such as *Ad Age* and companies such as the Landor Associates brand consulting firm. The annual report started in 2005, and the research includes 3 million consumers and 100,000 brands spanning thirty countries. The consumer-anchored perspective of this measure differentiates the index from others that tend to focus on a single metric or rely on expert opinion. BrandZ shows movement year over year for individual brands such as Coca-Cola, as well as for categories such as soft drinks. This index seeks to measure how brands appeal to customers by being meaningful, different, and salient.

Components of BrandZ's Brand Value:

- **Branded earnings:** A measurement of the portion of earnings for a firm that can be attributed to a specific brand; this information is procured through the study of annual reports and through other sources, such as Kantar Retail, a retail- and shopper-data insights and consulting business.

- **Brand multiple:** An estimate of future earnings potential for a brand; this is similar to valuation of stocks.
- **Brand contribution:** A measure of "the brand's uniqueness and its ability to stand out from the crowd, generate desire and cultivate loyalty" in the mind of the consumer; this measure seeks to understand price, availability, and distribution—factors that affect how relevant a brand is.[9] This part of the index focuses on how a brand is meaningful, different, and salient.

Type of measure: Millward Brown's BrandZ index combines financial metrics (branded earnings and brand multiple) with perception and behavior metrics (brand contribution).

Model:

Step 1: Determine the financial value of the brand:
- Branded earnings (amount of earnings attributed to a particular brand) × brand multiple = financial value of the brand

Step 2: Determine the brand contribution:
- A function of consumers' ratings on three factors that distinguish brands: meaningful, different, and salient

Step 3: Calculate the brand value:
- Financial value × brand contribution = brand value[10]

Interbrand Brand Valuation

Objective: Interbrand,[11] a well-known brand consultancy, seeks to understand the impact of brands on key stakeholders—a way to derive brand value. The Interbrand valuation methodology is one of the most widely referenced of all brand-value measures, and through the development of this methodology, this company helped develop the standard for requirements of monetary brand valuation.

The methodology was designed to incorporate market, brand, competitor, and financial data. Interbrand's analysis includes how the brand performs financially, how the brand affects purchase behavior, and the brand's competitive strength.

Components of Interbrand's Brand Valuation Technique

- **Financial analysis:** Based on economic profit, the "after-tax operating profit of the brand minus a charge for the capital used to generate the brand's revenue and margins"; intended to measure overall return.[12]
- **Role of branding index:** Derived from "primary research, a review of historical roles of brands for companies in that industry, or expert panel assessment" and expressed as a percentage of the portion of the purchase decision attributable to the brand.[13]

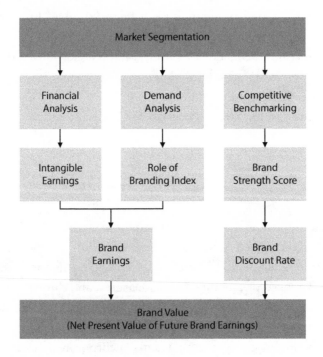

FIGURE AP 9.1 Model (Interbrand)

- **Brand strength:** Analysis of a brand in comparison to others in the industry and other world-class brands to measure the brand's ability to create loyal customers and sustainable demand. The ten factors used in this study are internal (clarity, commitment, protection, and responsiveness) and external (authenticity, relevance, differentiation, consistency, presence, and understanding).

Type of measure: Interbrand's Brand Valuation model is described as an "economic use" model for combining both brand equity and financial measures and "has become the most widely recognized and accepted methodology for brand valuation."[14] It combines financial metrics (financial analysis, role of branding index) and perception metrics (brand strength).

Brand Finance Royalty Relief[15]

Objective: Brand Finance uses a methodology called Royalty Relief to determine the value of brands; it measures the amount that a company would pay to license the brand if it were not a part of its portfolio. The company estimates future earnings for the brand and determines a royalty rate that would be charged for the brand. This index is often quoted by *Ad Age* and used by brand consultancies. The major components used to calculate the index—brand strength, royalty rate, and brand revenue—are typically available through public sources.

Components of Brand Finance's Technique

- **Brand strength index (BSI):** Calculated as a value between 0 and 100 and includes variables such as "emotional connection, financial performance, and sustainability."[16]

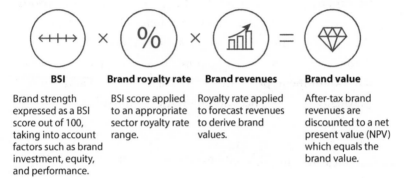

FIGURE AP 9.2 Model (Brand Finance Royalty Relief)

- **Brand royalty rate:** Determines the royalty range based on the licensing agreements of comparable brands within the industry.
- **Brand revenue:** Determines current and estimated future revenue attributable to the brand; future revenues are estimated based on historic revenues, analyst forecasts, and economic growth rates.

Type of measure: Brand Finance's valuation technique is primarily a financial metric (royalty rate, brand revenue). It does incorporate some amount of perception and/or behavior metrics, based on some of the variables within the BSI.

Y&R's BrandAsset Valuator (BAV)

Objective: Y&R's BrandAsset Valuator (BAV) was launched in 1993 in conjunction with professors from the Massachusetts Institute of Technology, Dartmouth, and Columbia. The BAV is the world's largest database of brand perceptions and includes evaluations from more than 1 million consumers. BAV considers key data points, relative to category competitors, to understand how brands gain and sustain momentum to create passion.[17]

The measure is featured in publications such as *Ad Age* and *Ad Week*. BAVLAB is a global consultancy that leverages BAV as its flagship product in discerning brand equity, custom research and tracking, and shopper insights.

Components of the BAV

- **Brand strength:** A combination of differentiation (the degree to which a brand is different and distinctive from other brands) and relevance (the degree to which a brand is appropriate for and connected to the consumer), viewed as an indicator of future performance
- **Brand stature:** A combination of esteem (the degree to which consumers hold a brand in high regard) and knowledge (the degree to which consumers are aware of a brand and understand what it offers), seen as a lagging indicator of brand health

Type of measure: Y&R's BAV is a measure of consumer knowledge and consumer perception that shows brands in relation to one another on a Power Grid (see model).

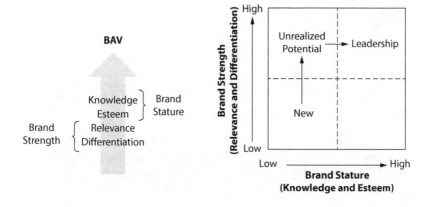

FIGURE AP 9.3 Model (BAV)

Net Promoter Score[18]

Objective: The Net Promoter Score (NPS), also known as "Net Promoter System," is a tool developed by Bain & Company and is most closely linked to Fred Reichheld, fellow and founder of the loyalty practice at the company. "Bain analysis shows that sustained value creators—companies that achieve long-term profitable growth—have Net Promoter Scores (NPS) two times higher than the average company. And Net Promoter System leaders on average grow at more than twice the rate of competitors."[19] This metric is also referred to as the "likelihood to recommend." Apple, American Express, and Delta are examples of companies using this methodology.

Components of the NPS Technique

NPS is based on a single question: *What is the likelihood that you would recommend Company X to a friend or colleague?* This question rated on a scale of 0 to 10 (see figure Ap 1.15), with 0 being "Not Likely at All" and 10 being "Extremely Likely."

- Promoters (9–10)
- Passives (7–8)
- Detractors (0–6)

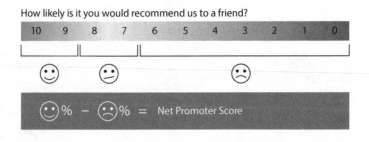

FIGURE AP 9.4 Model (NPS)

To calculate the NPS, subtract the number of Detractors from the number of Promoters. NPS practitioners are encouraged to follow up with open-ended questions to gain an understanding of the "why" behind the score.

Type of measure: This tool exclusively measures consumer behavior based on a customer's likelihood to recommend a product/business to friends.

Customer-Based Brand Equity Model[20]

Objective: The Customer-Based Brand Equity (CBBE) model was developed by Kevin Keller, a professor at the Tuck School of Business (Dartmouth). The belief behind the model was as follows: "In order to build a strong brand, you must shape how customers think and feel about your product. You have to build the right type of experiences around your brand, so that customers have specific, positive thoughts, feelings, beliefs, opinions, and perceptions about it. When you have strong brand equity, your customers will buy more from you, they'll recommend you to other people, they're more loyal, and you're less likely to lose them to competitors."[21]

Components of the CBBE Model

Keller's CBBE model contains four steps and six building blocks that he argues are imperative for building a successful brand:

- **Level 1:** Identity—salience, or awareness; who is the brand in the minds of the consumer?
- **Level 2:** Meaning—imagery, or how well your brand meets consumer needs on a social and psychological level; and performance, or how well your products meets the customers' physical needs.

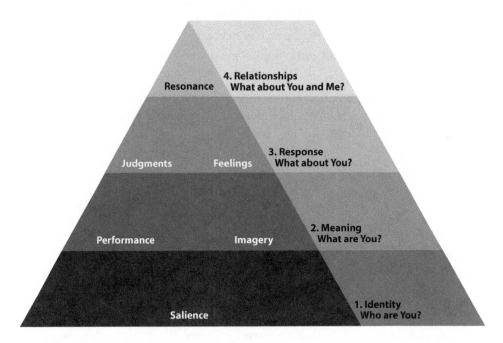

FIGURE AP 9.5 Model (Customer-Based Brand Equity Model).
Source: Keller, Kevin Lane (2013), *Strategic Brand Management: Building, Measuring, and Managing Brand Equity*, New York: Pearson Education.

- **Level 3:** Response—judgments, which fall into the categories of quality, credibility, consideration, and superiority; and feelings, either how a product makes consumers feel or how it makes consumers feel about themselves.
- **Level 4:** Relationships—resonance, which creates the following four categories: behavioral loyalty, attitudinal attachment, sense of community, and active engagement (strongest loyalty).

Type of measure: This measure is primarily focused on consumer perceptions of the brand.

The Harris Poll EquiTrend[22]

Objective: Since 1989, the Harris Poll EquiTrend has been examining brands and key indicators of performance. These elements include brand equity, consumer connection, and brand momentum. The output of the study is the equity score, measured as a numerical value and comparable across brands, industries, categories, and geographies. EquiTrend not only focuses on the total brand value, but also the individual drivers behind performance, and it identifies "rapid risers," or brands that have made the largest jump in equity score from the previous year. Georgetown University validated the methodology by confirming that brands with high ratings fared better during the 2008 economic downturn than those with low ratings.[23]

FIGURE AP 9.6 Model (EquiTrend).
Source: Harris Poll, "2019 Harris Poll EquiTrend Study," available from: https://the-harrispoll.com/equitrend/.

Components of the EquiTrend Technique

- **Familiarity:** How well do consumers know the brand?
- **Quality:** What is the impression that consumers have of the brand?
- **Consideration:** How do consumers want to interact with the brand?

"Harris Poll EquiTrend is based on a sample of U.S. consumers ages 15 and over surveyed online. Each respondent is asked to rate a total of 40 randomly selected brands out of 3,000+ brands in 300+ categories. Each brand receives approximately 1,000 ratings. Respondents are asked their familiarity with brands and rate the brands they are somewhat, very, or extremely familiar with. The data have been weighted to reflect the composition of U.S. residents age 15+."[24]

Type of measure: This index (illustrated in figure Ap 1.16) primarily measures consumer knowledge and consumer perceptions.

Harris Poll Reputation Quotient

Objective: The Harris Poll's Reputation Quotient (RQ), started in 1999, is an annual report measuring the public perception of brands. Metrics can help leaders discern future challenges and opportunities, manage their brand's reputation, and compare across competitors. "In RQ, we evaluate perceptions of corporate reputation and assess the relationship between reputational equity and supportive behaviors, such as trust in your company to do the right thing when faced with a product or service issue, willingness to say something positive, and intent to purchase or recommend your products and services."[25]

With more than fifteen years of data, brands can be compared year over year to understand the unique drivers of reputation. Public perceptions are tested across twenty attributes, which fall into the six component areas, listed next. To be considered for the Rating Phase, companies must first qualify through a Nomination Phase. The guide to scores is as follows: 80 and above: Excellent; 75–79: Very Good; 70–74: Good; 65–69: Fair; 55–64: Poor; 50–54: Very Poor; and Below 50: Critical. The top five companies from the 2020 report include Clorox Company, Hershey Company, Amazon, Publix Supermarkets, and General Mills.[26]

Components of RQ Technique

The respondents for this survey were selected from among those who have agreed to participate in Harris Poll and sample partner surveys in the past. Here are the areas in which respondents answered questions.

Social Responsibility - Supports good causes - Environmental responsibility - Community responsibility		Workplace Environment - Rewards employees fairly - Good place to work - Good employees
Vision & Leadership - Market opportunities - Excellent leadership - Clear vision for the future		Emotional Appeal - Feels good about - Admire and respect - Trust
Financial Performance - Outperforms competitors - Record or profitability - Low risk investment - Growth prospects		Products & Services - High quality - Innovative - Value for money - Stands behind

Type of measure: This is a perception metric.
   Model: See figure Ap 9.7 for a model.

Brand-Equity Monitor

Objective: As opposed to the other publicly available tools described in this appendix, a brand-equity monitor is a custom tool developed

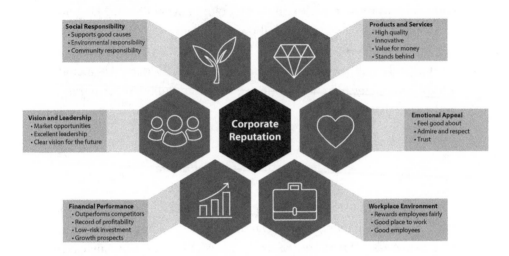

FIGURE AP 9.7 Model (RQ).
Source: Harris Poll (2019), "The 100 Most Visible Companies," available from: http://www.theharrispoll.com/reputation-quotient/.

to measure the attributes that matter most for a particular brand and category. Brand-equity monitors help marketers understand an aggregated and disaggregated view of the brand/category based on consumer perception, and they reflect the product's unique strategy and competitive environment. One of the most important aspects of developing a monitor is selecting the specific attributes that are tested. Monitors are either created in-house by a dedicated research team or contracted to an outside firm. This is typically one of the first things that a new chief marketing officer (CMO) will want to look at to understand the strengths, weaknesses, and in-market effectiveness of positioning efforts of the brands that they manage.

In the Buick example given in figure Ap 9.8 both functional and personality attributes are tested and compared to the segment average. The chart indicates that Buick falls significantly below the segment average on most attributes, while Lexus generally scores higher than the average. What this doesn't show is the progress that Buick has made over time on almost all these measures (another important aspect to measure), and it doesn't provide a comparison to other brands, such as Honda, Toyota, or Volkswagen, that may provide different insights.

Brand-Equity Monitor Components

Specific attributes in the report must be selected based on the brand, the desired positioning strategy, the competitors, and the marketplace. Deciding which attributes to measure can be exceptionally challenging.

Type of measure: Brand-equity monitors can measure both consumer knowledge and perception.

Example: See figure Ap 9.8 for an example.

Brand Attachment Model for Digital Interactions

As opposed to the measurement methods described previously, the brand attachment model varies in that (1) it is work in progress and not fully finished, and (2) it connects the consumer's perception of the brand with a unique type of consumer behavior—the degree of attachment to the brand.

This is a model that has been developed by three professors: William R. Dillon, Dave Singleton, and Piotr Dworak.[27] Academic models often tend to be more complex than practitioner models, but they also tend to be more complete. This new model shows promise in promoting better understanding of the connection between perception and behavior, particularly for digital interactions. Further, it helps to disentangle the complicated nature of consumer behavior by identifying dimensions of brand attachment.

Objective: This research is designed to help measure the impact of digital interactions and engagement. With marketers investing roughly 30 percent of their media on digital and consumers spending

Brand Imagery versus Luxury Makes

	Sept. 2013	Seg. Ave.	Acura	Buick	Infiniti	Lexus
High influence on purchase consideration ↑	Fits my personality	42	39	31	42	53
	Proud to own	52	46	35	53	65
	Willing to pay more	34	30	17	31	45
	Likely to notice ads	42	32	31	38	50
	Heard good things	53	50	41	54	71
	Value for the money	50	60	49	50	65
	Dependable	66	70	56	64	81
	Attractive styling	70	70	57	68	77
	Lasts a long time	62	62	50	58	77
Functional and Attachment	Safe	68	67	60	66	78
	Fuel efficient	44	53	43	46	56
	Retains its resale value	57	56	38	57	70
	Comfortable for the driver	72	70	64	68	85
	Fun to drive	67	64	47	65	73
	Responsive handling	68	64	54	67	78
	Luxurious	70	57	46	73	82
	Environmentally friendly	45	47	40	44	55
	Quality materials, fit, and finish	72	68	54	71	83
Low influence on purchase consideration ↓	Prestigious	69	55	41	67	79
	Quick acceleration	64	60	42	63	73
	Advanced features	71	66	52	70	83
	Customer-oriented dealerships	58	55	48	55	74
High influence on purchase consideration ↑	Innovative	34	31	20	38	44
	Trusted	44	49	50	36	56
	Confident	43	39	36	40	54
	Exciting	37	27	19	36	39
	Passionate	28	20	17	27	25
Personality	Arrogant	19	5	6	13	18
	Responsible	35	42	41	30	44
Low influence on purchase consideration ↓	Distinctive	44	29	28	38	50
	Practical	31	45	60	27	35
	Adventurous	30	19	11	24	27
	Aggressive	22	14	8	15	17

☐ Significantly above segment average   ☐ Significantly below segment average

FIGURE AP 9.8 Luxury Image Perceptions versus Segment Brand Average, September 2013.

Data source: Adapted from a General Motors document in Wells, D. Graham, Kimberly A. Whitler, and Gerry Yemen (2016), "Buick at a Crossroads: Building Brand Momentum," *UVA-M-0907*, Charlottesville, VA: Darden Business Publishing. Notes: Luxury makes with Buick: $n = 450$.

Functional and Attachment imagery: How well do these characteristics apply to (make)? (Percentage that definitely/probably applies among very/somewhat familiar)

Personality imagery: How well do these characteristics apply to (make)? Check all that apply.

(Percentage of "yes" replies among very/somewhat familiar)

roughly six hours per day engaging with digital media, understanding how to measure the consumer's perception and behavior related to digital media exposure is growing in importance.[28]

Brand Attachment Model Components

This model provides specific measures—the left two columns represent perceptions of the brand that the consumer has, and the right

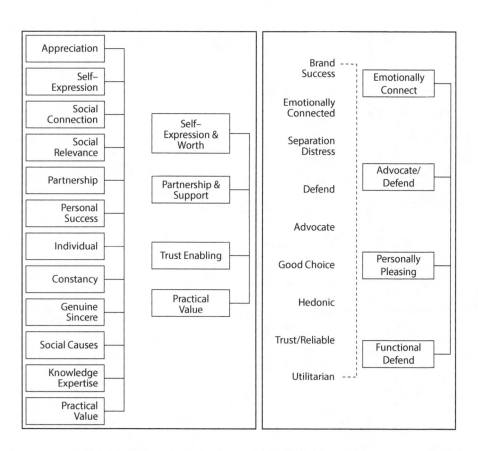

FIGURE AP 9.9 Model (brand attachment model for digital interactions)
Source: William R. Dillon, used with permission

two columns represent attributes that describe consumer behavior and attachment to the brand.

Type of measure: The model measures both brand perception and an aspect of consumer behavior.

PULLING IT TOGETHER

10

Activating Brand Tools through Practice and Implementation

WHY DO MARKETERS EXIST? How do they contribute above and beyond all other functions? The book started by asking these questions and introduced the marketing impact framework. The answer is simple in theory—marketers exist to help create positional advantage that drives profitable growth for a firm or brand over time. Therefore, the unique skill that marketers should bring to a firm is the ability to combine market insight (e.g., about consumers and competitors) with the firm's capability to define the strategies and plans to help companies achieve positional, brand and financial advantage.

However, theory is simply a notion of how the world should work. How to transform theories into action and results in practice is often elusive. When I first joined Procter & Gamble (P&G), I didn't really know how to lead a business to achieve sustained levels of growth. I didn't understand the tools, methods, or practices that could be employed to do so. My academic education (both undergraduate and graduate levels) had provided me with foundational skills: strategic, conceptual, and analytical thinking. I knew that brands mattered, that differentiation was good, and that creating a strategic vision was critical.

I didn't know how to disaggregate a brand into its component parts; how to compare the positioning of one brand to a competitive brand to determine which would, *ceteris paribus*, have the greater likelihood to win in the marketplace; how to develop a sound strategic plan; or how to ensure that the strategies could be executed for superior in-market impact. I simply was lost in the theory-doing gap. However, I was fortunate that, over decades, I had opportunities to learn from others, from trial and error, and from continuing education, research, and investigation.

My hope is that this book has demystified marketing and addressed the theory-doing gap by introducing a number of tools that can help marketers convert theory into effective practice. The book followed the marketing impact framework process (in chapter 1) and introduced three marketing strategy tools in chapters 2–4 that help marketers understand how to define and communicate desired positioning: the positioning concept, brand essence statement (BES), and strategy maps. Chapters 5 and 6 introduced bridging tools designed to help marketers span the strategy and planning divide (i.e., strategic marketing plan, creative brief). Chapters 7–9 then introduced three marketing planning tools: the MarTech Blueprint, influencer mapping tool, and methods for measuring brands. In aggregate, the book is designed to help aspiring C-level executives better understand and leverage marketing for growth.

Putting the Tools to Work

Because this book is focused on not only driving awareness, but actually building skill, it is important to develop proficiency. Just as surveys or statistical methods are tools that can help marketers make better decisions, knowing how to effectively use a tool with skill requires practice. One of the experiences I most valued from my time at P&G was their emphasis on practicing using different tools in environments where it didn't matter (e.g., brown bag lunches) so that when you did apply the tool in situations where it mattered, there was a degree of competency that increased the likelihood of success. This final chapter is designed to improve implementation success by providing exercises to help you practice using the tools to ensure that when you put them to the test for real, you can have greater confidence in the results.

Concept Positioning Statement

The value of writing—and testing— positioning concept statements over and over again is that at some point, you will become more adept at predicting which statement will resonate best with consumers. This skill is incredibly important. For example, when I stepped into a chief marketing officer (CMO) role for a large, *Fortune* 500 company, I reviewed the strategic positioning reflected in their marketing communications and found that it was weak. If the starting point of the brand—the core positioning—is weak, then every dollar invested to communicate that positioning is largely wasted. While my experience writing and testing hundreds of concept tests had prepared me to be able to reverse engineer and assess this particular company's positioning, I didn't simply rely on my experience. Rather, I ran a series of quantitative tests (similar to the ones described in chapter 2) to generate actual target consumer insight and test my hypotheses. In this case, the results validated my assessment. But this was possible only because I had spent years writing, testing, and measuring concepts in different categories and for different target consumers.

There are three steps to building skill in developing positioning concept statements. The first step is to find an advertisement and reverse engineer the positioning behind the ad using the problem-solution-support framework described in chapter 2. In other words, find a print ad from a magazine (often the easiest to find) that has body copy, and then identify the problem, solution, and support that are being communicated in the ad. To develop better capability, write a few versions of statements and have a number of marketers judge which one most accurately reflects the ad. Do this over and over again until you can look at an ad and almost immediately reverse engineer the positioning reflected.

Once you have developed some competency at reverse engineering existing ads, the next step is to find two competing ads in the same category and assess which is stronger. Specifically, go through the same reverse engineering exercise and assess which ad has the strongest positioning based on your understanding of the target audience. For example, in 2017, Sprint and Verizon ran commercials during the Super Bowl that were consistent with each brand's long-term positioning. Find the two commercials online and then reverse engineer the positioning. Whose position is stronger—and for whom—and why? What are their concepts, and which has a more compelling, differentiated, consumer-relevant positioning? In this case, each brand did an excellent job of effectively communicating its core positioning in a way that would resonate with different segments of the market.

The third step is to develop positioning concept statements from scratch. There are two ways to do this: (1) pick a brand, write the current positioning statement, and think about how you could strengthen and improve it; and/or (2) create a new brand positioning for that brand from scratch. This second option is much harder. Essentially, you have to identify a "white-space" opportunity and come up with a brand that would fill that gap. Consider the following example of a new product problem statement:

> I always feel more professional when I wear heels, as I know that they look better with my suits. Unfortunately, there isn't a high-heeled shoe that looks professional and is comfortable to walk or stand in for any amount of time. I have to trade looks for comfort. I wish there were a brand that could create high heels that are as comfortable as slippers but look as polished as the best designer brands.

Take this problem statement and complete it. What different ideas can you create that solve this problem? And what types of proof might be most compelling? If this example doesn't resonate with you, pick something from your brand that you know is a pain point for consumers. For example, when I worked in the food category, consumers were shifting to more grab-and-go food options. I could write a problem statement centered on this idea and then develop options for solution statements. The last place you can look to practice developing positioning concept statements is to reflect on your own experiences as a consumer. The example given here is one that is based on my own experience as a professor. I often have to stand for several hours, and yet there aren't nice-looking high-heeled shoes for women that are also comfortable (hint: a big opportunity for entrepreneurs).

Regardless of the inspiration you use to practice writing and evaluating positioning concept statements, this skill will help you not only become more adept at identifying optimal positioning territories, but also think about which new innovation opportunities should deliver higher levels of growth. It is a powerful skill that can be beneficial throughout your career—but it requires continual practice.

Brand Essence Statement

Once you've developed some proficiency at reverse engineering and constructing positioning concept statements, it is time to start practicing developing BESs. You will find that these two skills go together. They are related concepts, as the positioning concept statement defines the general territory, and the BES provides greater specificity around the attribute choices.

While there are a number of ways to disaggregate brands into their component parts, choose one of the formats provided in chapter 3 (e.g., Parthenon, dog bone, or pyramid) or one from your own firm to perform this next practice: convert a number of print ads from Coca-Cola into BESs. The first ad is vintage (figure 10.1), the second is more contemporary (figure 10.2), and the third is an ad for a new product launched this year (figure 10.3). What is the rational benefit

FIGURE 10.1 Ice-cold Coca-Cola ad; used with permission

that Coke stands for in each ad? What is the proof of the rational benefit (e.g., reasons to believe)? And what is the emotional benefit? What personality is being communicated, and what can you sense about their brand values? Most importantly, how has the brand evolved over time? What has remained constant, and what has changed? Why do you think the brand leaders made these changes? As you convert the ads into BESs, remember three important points:

1. Aspects of the BES may be communicated in copy (i.e., "Delicious and Refreshing" in figure 10.1), and also through visual cues (i.e., bottles lying in snow). You have to look at the totality of the ad to try to deconstruct the brand into its constituent parts.

FIGURE 10.2 "Coke side of life" ad; used with permission

2. It is unlikely that an entire BES can be completely filled out by looking at just one ad. Brand values often aren't communicated through ads. Emotional benefits are also less common in print ads. It is difficult to communicate all aspects of a BES in a single print ad. That is why it is helpful to look at the totality of a brand's communications (e.g., television, radio, billboard, digital, print, press releases, etc.). If in doubt,

FIGURE 10.3 Coca-Cola with Coffee ad; used with permission

always leave that section of the BES blank. For example, in the ad shown in figure 10.1, there isn't clarity around an emotional benefit, so I'd leave that section of the BES blank (or put a question mark there).

3. Don't force an answer. When I work with various executive groups, we often feel compelled to fill in all the blanks. When I provide a BES template, executives want to put something in every box. When I did this exercise as a general manager/ CMO, if the majority of the individuals in the room completing the BES didn't get the exact same answer, we would leave it as a question mark. The reason is simple. We are trying to identify a brand's strategy by analyzing communications that are presumably based on the strategy. If it isn't clear to a majority of experts, then it isn't clear at all. You can't then assume that you are correctly identifying the strategy.

Once you've identified the brand architecture, assess it. Why do you think that the brand is being communicated as cold and refreshing? Why did the brand leaders choose that specific benefit to communicate? Who do you think the target audience is and why? Do you think that this BES is strong? Why or why not? Do you think that it would resonate with target consumers?

The point of this exercise is twofold. First, you want to practice converting the output of a BES (i.e., print ad or marketing communication) into the brand strategy against which the ad or communication was conceived. Second, and equally important, you should start thinking deeper about what makes a strong BES. Why is one BES, *ceteris paribus*, better than another? The thinking side of this exercise is what will ultimately separate marketers. It is one thing to understand the BES, but quite another to develop the skill of assessing whether the BES is compelling.

Next, identify the brand architecture of the Coca-Cola ads in figures 10.2 and 10.3. These are more contemporary ads than the one in figure 10.1. Assume that each of these ads reflects the brand architecture at the time that it was run. Of course, in reality, this would be problematic. To fully understand a brand's architecture, you would want to assess all the related communication vehicles because a single ad might not convey an important element of the strategy. For this exercise, however, assume that each ad represents the Coca-Cola brand of that particular era. How has the brand evolved over time? Has the target consumer changed? Or do you think that what the brand desires to stand for has changed?

Once you have gone through this process, consider Pepsi. If Coca-Cola owned the benefit of "refreshing," how should Pepsi compete? What is vulnerable about the BES ?How might you be able to develop a competing brand strategy?

Finally, to continue to develop your skill, take the print ads from the positioning concept statement exercise you did earlier in this chapter and create BESs for each brand. Look at the BESs next to the positioning concept statements and critique them. Do certain brands appear to be positioned to gain a greater portion of the market (i.e., have they chosen positions and brand strategies that are likely to have more mass appeal)? Why? How is each brand vulnerable? If you were competing in these categories, how would you try to grow your brand? What would that BES look like?

Finally, once you've developed comfort and proficiency in looking at print ads, record a television show or two and watch all the commercials that go along with them. Who is the target? What is the BES? How are they positioned within the industry? Over time, and with practice, you will be able to do this in your head. But when you start, writing it down on a piece of paper and analyzing it will be help you get to the point where you can do it in real time.

Strategy Maps

There are a number of ways to become more proficient at developing strategy maps. As a starting point, I recommend developing a library of strategy maps that you believe are useful as decision-making tools and effective as communication tools. As you come across examples at work, make copies and file them. In this first stage, you are becoming aware of the way in which others in your organization use strategy maps to make decisions and sell a point of view. This heightened awareness—which includes identifying, assessing, and deciding the ones that are effective—is helpful in developing a skill. Any time you are reading or observing a presentation, pay specific attention to valuable strategy maps and add them to your file too.

Once you are more attuned to strategy maps, begin trying to develop them as part of a presentation. Look for opportunities to use an illustration, rather than words, to communicate positioning, industry-level metrics, and so forth. Follow the steps outlined in chapter 4 as you practice developing these maps.

If you happen to work with a consulting firm, I recommend that you invite somebody from that firm to walk you through a tutorial on the strategy maps that they use, the conditions under which they use them, and other factors. Often, the primary benefit of hiring a consulting firm is their ability to convert information into strategy maps that drive decision-making and alignment. Whenever possible, tap into this expertise.

As you can see, the primary method to gain proficiency in using strategy maps is first through awareness, observation, and assessment, and then through practice. Over time, you will transition from being a passive consumer of strategy maps—without much cognitive assessment or engagement—to becoming an active identifier and utilizer of effective strategy maps.

Strategic Marketing Plan

To become adept at strategic planning, one way to begin is to practice using it in your personal life. It is often easier to create personal strategic plans and doing so will help you better understand how to use this tool before applying it to work situations. There are two key benefits to starting with personal strategic plans rather than business plans: (1) they are easier to develop because you typically have most, if not all, of the information you need, so you don't have to do additional research and insight generation; and (2) when you put your plan into action, you will understand almost immediately whether the plan was effective. In many cases, our strategic plans are too complicated or too much for the available resources. The result is poor execution. By practicing developing and implementing strategic plans in your personal life, you will understand the consequences of being decisive and identifying weak strategies, tactics, and measures. This will provide important insights when you then apply the tool in your work. Here are a few ideas for practicing developing and implementing strategic plans:

- Financial plan: Develop a strategic plan to save for some particular event (e.g., holiday, vacation, car, etc.).
- Retirement plan: Develop a strategic plan to prepare all aspects of life (e.g., mental, physical, financial, spiritual, etc.) for retirement.
- Health plan: Develop a plan to achieve better health outcomes.
- Work-related learning plan: Develop a strategic plan to create a competency at something new at work (e.g., learn about blockchain or another contemporary issue).
- Child college development plan: Develop a plan that identifies the key strategies, tactics, and measures that will help focus you or your kids on the preparation needed to achieve college aspirations.
- General learning plan: Develop a strategic plan to create a competency that is not related to work (e.g., learn a new dance, a new language, or a new instrument).

To practice developing the tool and assessing whether it is effective, you want to make the time horizon less than a year. The vision may be longer, but as described here, keep the balance of the plan within a year. This is important because it will allow you to (1) measure your outcome relative to the goal (i.e., whether you achieved success); and

(2) reflect on whether you needed to use all the available tactics or whether some were unnecessary and others more important. In fact, if you want to pick an even shorter period of time (i.e., three months) to make the practice more vivid, feel free to do so.

To learn how to develop effective strategic plans, it is helpful for you to experience a less-than-optimal plan—one that isn't as well thought out as it needs to be. If you develop three strategic plans for financial health, physical health, and learning and have a combined total of forty tactics, do you think that you actually need all that to accomplish your goals? No. When you can feel and experience the impact of plans that aren't well done, then you are more likely to be rigorous in your choice of strategies and tactics in the future.

When I first learned about strategic marketing plans (I was about twenty-four), I immediately went home and developed a financial goal that I wanted to achieve by age thirty. I drafted a number of strategies and tactics and put the plan aside. A few days later, I brushed if off and challenged myself to identify the fewest number of tactics that would enable me to accomplish the goal. The primary strategy was related to cutting unnecessary spending to allow a higher level of saving. The most important tactic was to "pay myself first each month"—immediately take money out of my checking account and put it in savings, which I then never touched. The second most important tactic was to identify the key ways that I could make the biggest cuts to my monthly spending without sacrificing quality of life. I then put the plan away and looked at it again a few days later.

At this point, I thought I had a strong plan, so I put it into practice. Within the first month, I immediately saw the benefit of developing a strategic plan—I was much more disciplined in my behavior. Because monthly progress/measurement (i.e., via a spreadsheet) was a part of my strategic plan, I was able to see the progress toward my goal each month—important interim steps that enabled me to see the payoff from my investment. The discipline used in developing and then implementing this plan enabled me to be able to achieve my financial goal two years ahead of schedule.

While this is just one example, I have used this tool on a number of occasions to help achieve personal and professional goals that are beyond the scope of managing a business—typically when I have a vision that is distant (e.g., retirement) and I know that to achieve that vision, I have to take a number of progressive steps over time. In other words, achieving the goal requires a multiyear, multistep process. I've found that planning is critical in these cases because without it, I have little chance of "lucking into" accomplishing the vision. Without a financial plan for retirement, I won't just wake up at age sixty-five and have enough money saved. Without a strategic plan for achieving better health, I know I won't just wake up and be the healthiest version of myself. Not only is this tool beneficial for managing a business, but it can significantly help in managing other professional (i.e., career) and personal goals as well.

Once you've practiced using this tool in your personal life, begin applying it at work. If you don't have an annual plan, convert your "project list" into a strategic plan. This isn't easy, and it will take time. Once you've done this, share it with your boss and other key stakeholders. Get their feedback. At least monthly, review and update the strategic plans you've developed. For them to be effective, it is important to review your progress and adapt your plans to the current circumstances.

Creative Brief

If you haven't used some version of a creative brief before, there are a number of ways to start practicing. One method would be similar to the reverse engineering approach used to practice developing a positioning concept statement or BES. Look at the Buick print ad shown in figure 10.4 and write the creative brief that you think would have led to it.

This will take some time, but try to identify the brief that would have been the basis for the ad. Share your brief with an account

FIGURE 10.4 Buick ad; used with permission

manager or planner at an ad agency. See if they agree. Have a discussion over what they might change.

You can use this method to practice. Convert a number of print ads into the creative brief that would have generated each ad. Once this becomes fairly easy, fill out a brief for any project that you are working on—whether it is an information technology (IT) project, a creative project, or even a media project. Practice using the tool by completing a task and then getting feedback. For example, assume that you are working on a technology integration project. Complete a draft of some version of the creative brief. Next, seek feedback from others working on the project, which can include technologists or even external vendors. Is the brief clear? Are those who have to do the work clear on what their roles are and what success looks like?

I also recommend that you ask your creatives (either external or internal) to assess the version of the creative brief that your company uses. If you work with an external agency, ask them to evaluate your format versus other firms. Which is most effective, and why? Which is least effective? If they could improve your creative brief format, what would they change? Invite them to lunch and have them conduct a tutorial on better and worse creative briefs. Further, ask the creatives about the projects they worked on that (1) were the most motivating, and (2) had the best in-market results. Try to understand what drove the motivation and the impact. Ask them to show you the creative briefs from which the work emerged.

Essentially, the objective of these exercises is to enable you to understand the types of creative briefs that exist and how the users of the brief perceive the different versions, and to think more deeply about the tool that you and your team are currently using. Is there an opportunity to make the creative brief more effective? If so, how?

The Marketing Technology Blueprint

The MarTech Blueprint will be the most challenging of the tools to practice, primarily because you can't find publicly available data from other companies. Consequently, you must use information from your current company to practice with. To begin, ask peers in technology, operations, and other data-customer interfacing functions for any technology maps that they might have. The easiest place to start is with something that already exists. If your organization already has a MarTech Blueprint—or if other functions have a technology map for their functioning—begin by analyzing those that already exist. How was each one created? For what purpose? And by whom? How has it been useful, and what are its limitations?

After you've spent significant time looking at examples from within your firm, then begin to develop a MarTech Blueprint for a specific, finite-sized territory. In other words, just map a single interface to be able to start small. It's more important that you understand how it this is done, and starting simple will be easier. For example, take the email marketing system. Map the related systems, technologies, interfaces, and other elements on a single piece of paper. Look at alternative ways to illustrate the relationships. Is one way clearer and easier to understand than another? It may be helpful to seek feedback from others, particularly those in technology. Understand the degree to which you have accurately and completely captured the email marketing system. Ask your colleagues in technology who are adept at developing technology blueprints what opportunities exist to strengthen your blueprint. Should you simplify or make it more efficient?

Over time, with practice, you can extend your blueprint to encompass all consumer-facing interfaces. The best way to become proficient is to work with and learn from those who are highly skilled—typically your colleagues in technology. See if you can collaborate on the development of a blueprint or lead a specific project with their counsel. In a set of interviews that I conducted with the CMO and chief information officer (CIO) of Regal Entertainment Cinemas, they talked at length about several steps they took to ensure that the marketing organization became skilled in MarTech:

1. The CMO added a technologist to the marketing organization so that the vocabulary and language permeated the organization (in addition to improving MarTech project success).

2. The CMO and CIO held weekly scrums with their organizations (i.e., stand-up meetings) to talk about key marketing technology projects.
3. The CMO and CIO (and their organizations) collaborated on annual, strategic plans, as well as more project-based plans.

The CEO of Regal Entertainment Cinemas believed that firm-level success required terrific marketing-IT collaboration, so the CMO and CIO were incentivized (had shared goals and expectations) and expected to work together—and they did.[1] As you can imagine, the CMO often sounded like a technologist and the CIO often sounded like a marketer. By collaborating, they had begun to adopt the other's language and skills.

Key Opinion Leader and Influencer Mapping

An effective method to learn how to develop an influencer map is to engineer such a map from an existing program. For example, identify an internal or external program that has achieved significant publicity. Gather insight into what the influencer program entailed, and then do your best, based on available data, to map an existing program. Once you have mapped it, step back and critically assess it. Does the influencer program appear to align clearly with the brand strategy? Does the choice of influencers support the strategy? How about influencer engagement? Does it support the strategy, or are there gaps? If you were in charge of the influencer program, what would you keep? What would you do differently? Why?

To practice, consider the Lyft Influencer program of 2018.[2] The ride-sharing company set as a goal to be one of the most mentioned brands across social media channels (relative to sponsored posts). To do this, they used a wide mix of celebrity (e.g., Zayn Malik and Snoop Dogg) and micro influencers (e.g., Bryan Abasolo and Peyton Mabry, who access smaller, niche audiences). Using more than 1,000 influencers, Lyft achieved 5.9 million engagements in one year—an impressive feat for a car service.

Brand Measurement Methods

To practice using insight from chapter 9, on brand measurement methods, compile all the methods that your company uses to measure brand strength. Identify what is being measured (e.g., consumer perception, consumer behavior, financial health). Connect the various measures using the framework provided in chapter 9. To what extent is your company measuring all the facets of brand health? Do the specific measures make sense—do they connect directly to the BES and strategic marketing plan? Are there gaps in understanding?

To begin thinking more deeply about brand health, a good starting point is to assess your company's measurement of the brand. Often, marketers inherit the measurement programs that somebody else created. It is critical to take the necessary time to assess whether these measures are complete, useful, and helpful in strategic decision-making; in other words, don't assume that the measurement systems are sufficient, complete, or accurate.

When I became a general manager/CMO, I found that across the different companies, we generally didn't do a great job of measuring brand health. More important, we did not link it to business and financial outcomes. At one firm, I partnered with the chief financial officer (CFO) to codevelop and measure marketing performance (including brand health). This was possible only because I had a strong relationship with the CFO and trusted him. We both wanted to make sure that marketing was as effective and efficient as possible, and in many cases, the databases that I needed to access to measure marketing were controlled by finance. It simply required collaboration. If you are fortunate enough to have a finance/IT partnership like this, I recommend collaborating in order to assess your current brand measurement approach and identify opportunities for improvement.

An Opportunity to Practice Using These Tools in an Integrated Manner

The exercises thus far have focused on individual tools. For this next exercise, the goal will be to explore, in a more integrated way, how the tools can work together. Figure 10.5 shows a print ad from Olay. Start by reverse engineering the positioning concept and BES. Assuming that this ad is reflective of the brand, how is the brand positioned and what is the essence of this brand? Considering what you know about

FIGURE 10.5 Olay ad; used with permission

skin care (or what you have found out after doing a little research), how might you place the brands/consumers on a strategy map? As a suggestion, create a strategy map that reflects the brand positions of three skin products leading in market share—Olay, Neutrogena, and L'Oreal. Look up ads for each and think about how you might represent the different brand positions. Next, think about what the Olay brand is trying to stand for. Although you don't have any business information, what types of marketing strategies might activate this brand and help solidify it in the minds of consumers? Finally, identify the creative brief against which this ad was created. Now step back and look at the relationship between the positioning concept, the BES, the strategy map, the strategic marketing plan, and the creative brief. These are the key tools—and the process—that enable marketers to identify, create, and bring a brand to life.

A Few Thoughts on Implementation at the Team or Department Level

Up to this point, I have focused on helping you gain proficiency and skill at using and applying these marketing tools as an individual. However, you may manage a team or department, and a key question that I often get relates to how to tool up a team or department. In other words, if you inherit a department and there isn't a sophisticated approach to marketing in place, how do you lead a transformation that will improve your staff's skill and capability?

The short answer is that this will depend on a lot of factors, such as the current skill level of the department, the gaps, the industry within which you are competing, your degree of managerial discretion (i.e., how much latitude you have to implement transformation), the appetite for transformative change that the CEO and C-suite have, the expectations of the department, and so forth.

While I won't attempt to cover the territory that transformation books explore (there are numerous books on the topic of leading transformative change), I will offer a few thoughts on how to shift departmental skills. The starting point is training. Pick one central tool that you think will be most beneficial and identify opportunities to train the entire department on it. For example, assume that you want to start with the BES. Have the entire department read the chapter in this book on this topic, and then conduct a workshop whereby you lead the team through the conversion process described earlier in this chapter.

Holding biweekly or monthly training sessions can do a lot more than just improve tool proficiency. It can help strengthen departmental camaraderie and signal a firm-level commitment to invest in employees, resulting in stronger dedication and loyalty from them in turn. These benefits can transcend individual- and group-level marketing capability. The easy starting point is to focus on building ability through investment in training and then incorporating the tools into departmental processes.

A Concluding Note

I will share one final story to help make both the importance of the tools and the implementation of them more vivid. After I learned how to develop and use strategic marketing plans, I found myself at one point in charge of marketing strategy at the leading retailer in our category. At the C-level, we had a terrific strategic plan for the firm, but none of the individual functions had a strategic plan. After having worked at a company where everybody had a strategic plan—so all the work was integrated to achieve departmental and firm-level goals—it seemed to me that functions at my new firm were operating at cross-purposes. There wasn't any synchronization of action across the functions to achieve the firm-level strategic plan. In the marketing department, a primary cross-functional partner was merchandising. When I arrived at the firm, the merchants didn't like the marketers and vice versa. I believed that part of the problem was that our work wasn't aligned.

I asked the merchants for their strategic plans. They didn't have any. They had numerical goals, but no codified, written document that explained how they planned to deliver those goals. My department didn't have any plans either. Consequently, I conducted training to help my department understand how to develop strategic plans, and then we spent a couple of months interviewing the merchants and essentially creating strategic plans for them. This enabled us to do a better job of creating our own strategic plans that would align with the merchants' goals. Importantly, it helped the merchants understand that the marketers weren't evil—both functions were operating in a poor planning system that was creating frustration and conflict.

If you are as I was in my first general management marketing role—a fish out of water—then I hope that this book has helped you understand *why you matter* (marketers help drive growth) and how to develop greater marketing skill. It is a starting point to help all marketers, regardless of academic education or company experience, learn about the basic tools that can provide a common structure and approach with which to tackle marketing roles. I hope that this book enables you to understand some foundational tools, begin putting them into practice, and inspires you to continue learning about these advanced methods.

Notes

1. The Marketing Impact Framework

1. Kimberly A. Whitler, "How These 15 Firms Better Prepare Marketers to Become CEOs: Insight from the C-Suite," *Forbes*, January 20, 2019, available from: https://www.forbes.com/sites/kimberlywhitler/2019/01/20/why-these-15-firms -are-better-at-preparing-marketers-to-become-ceos-insight-from-the-c-suite /#26dd5e8745c0.

2. Marketing Science Institute, "5 Things I Know About Marketing—John Deighton, Harvard Business School," MSI.org, available from: http://www.msi .org/articles/5-things-i-know-about-marketing-john-deighton-harvard-business -school/, accessed 2017.

3. Kimberly A. Whitler, "Survey Reveals the Companies That Develop the Best C-Level Marketers," *Forbes*, August 21, 2016, available from: https://www.forbes.com /sites/kimberlywhitler/2016/08/21/best-companies-for-developing-c-level-marketing -leaders/.

4. Kimberly A. Whitler and Neil Morgan, "Why CMOs Never Last and What to Do About It," *Harvard Business Review* 95 (July–August 2017): 45–54.

5. Whitler, "Survey Reveals the Companies."

6. Whitler, "How These 15 Firms Better Prepare Marketers."

7. Kimberly A. Whitler, "Study Results: The Top Companies That Prepare Marketers to Become CEOs," *Forbes*, January 12, 2019, available from:

https://www.forbes.com/sites/kimberlywhitler/2019/01/12/study-results-the-top-companies-that-prepare-marketers-to-become-ceos/#320357315c1c.

8. Procter & Gamble, "About Us," Procter & Gamble, available from: https://news.pg.com/about/core_strengths.

9. There are several foundational resources that help provide insights into marketing's contribution to a firm. For a sample, see Kevin Lane Keller and Vanitha Swaminathan, *Strategic Brand Management: Building, Measuring, and Managing Brand Equity* (Harlow, UK: Pearson Education Ltd., 2019); Phillip Kotler, *Marketing Management*, (Englewood Cliffs, NJ: Pearson Education, 2000); Edmund Jerome McCarthy, *Marketing: A Managerial Approach*, (Homewood, IL: Irwin, 1960); and Neil A. Morgan "Marketing and Business Performance," *Journal of Academy of Marketing Science*, 40 (2019): 102–119.

2. The Positioning Concept

1. Author interview with Lee Susen (September 9, 2016).

2. John T. Gourville, "Eager Sellers and Stony Buyers: Understanding the Psychology of New-Product Adoption," *Harvard Business Review*, June 2019, 1–9.

3. Jodi Helmer, "Inside a College Entrepreneur's Unique Coat Check Business," *Entrepreneur*, June 1, 2013, available from: https://www.entrepreneur.com/article/226384.

4. Kimberly A. Whitler, "Survey Reveals the Companies That Develop the Best C-Level Marketing Leaders," *Forbes*, August 21, 2015, available from: https://www.forbes.com/sites/kimberlywhitler/2016/08/21/best-companies-for-developing-c-level-marketing-leaders/#5f4702464c31.

5. While there are many positioning concept development and testing processes in practice, this book outlines a process that any marketing organization—large or small—could employ. In addition, while this book refers to "products" throughout, the same process can be employed to develop new services, ideas, experiences, and so on.

6. Gourville, "Eager Sellers and Stony Buyers."

7. Joan Schneider and Julie Hall, "Why Most Product Launches Fail," *Harvard Business Review*, April 2011, available from: https://hbr.org/2011/04/why-most-product-launches-fail.

8. Minda Zetlin, "Advice from the 23-Year-Old Who Said No to Mark Cuban," *Inc.*, February 1, 2013, available from: http://www.inc.com/minda-zetlin/advice-from-the-23-year-old-who-said-no-to-mark-cuban.html.

3. The Brand Essence Statement

1. Rita Clifton, *Brands and Branding*, the *Economist* series, 2nd ed. (Bloomberg Press, 2009), 7.

2. Noel Tichy, "J.C. Penney and the Terrible Costs of Hiring an Outsider CEO," *Fortune*, November 13, 2014, available from: http://fortune.com/2014/11/13/jc-penney-ron-johnson-ceo-succession/; and Dana Mattioli, "Penney Ousts President," *Wall Street Journal*, June 19, 2012, available from: http://www.wsj.com/articles/SB10001424052702303836404577474931017078226.

3. David A. Aaker, *Managing Brand Equity: Capitalizing on the Value of a Brand Name* (New York: Free Press, 1991), 7.

4. Axios Harris Poll 100 (2019), "2019 Corporate Reputation Rankings," Harris Poll, available from: https://theharrispoll.com/axios-harrispoll-100/.

5. Akane Otani, "America's Most Loved and Most Hated Companies," *Bloomberg*, February 5, 2015, available from: http://www.bloomberg.com/news/articles/2015-02-05/america-s-most-loved-and-most-hated-companies (accessed September 21, 2015).

6. Chief Executive (2012), "Goldman Sachs: A Cautionary Tale in Branding," Chief Executive Group, available from: http://chiefexecutive.net/goldman-sachs-a-cautionary-tale-in-branding/.

7. Kimberly A. Whitler, "Believers vs. Non-Believers: Convincing Internal Partners That Marketing Can Help Drive Business," *Forbes*, September 10, 2011, available from: http://www.forbes.com/sites/kimberlywhitler/2011/09/10/the-believers-versus-the-non-believers-convincing-internal-partners-that-marketing-can-help-drive-business-results/#21f240e13ad8.

8. Kimberly A. Whitler, "Developing a Superior Strategic Marketing Plan," in *UVA-M-0890* (Charlottesville, VA: Darden Business Publishing, 2015).

9. Kimberly A. Whitler and Marian Chapman Moore, "Market Definition, Segmentation, and Targeting: Three (of Four) Steps in Developing Marketing Strategy," in *UVA-M-0895* (Charlottesville, VA: Darden Business Publishing, 2015).

10. Otani, "America's Most Loved and Most Hated Companies."

11. Jack Linshi, "This Chart Shows How Comcast's Business Is Changing Forever," *Time*, May 4, 2015, available from: http://time.com/3845271/comcast-internet-tv-subscribers/.

12. If this topic interests you, see Kevin Keller, *Strategic Brand Management*, 4th ed. (Englewood Cliffs, NJ: Pearson, 2015).

13. "About PetSmart," PetSmart, available from: https://www.petsmartcorporate.com/.

14. "Welcome to the PetSmart Charities Newsroom," PetSmart Charities, available from: https://www.petsmartcharities.org/media/media-kit.

15. "Welcome to the PetSmart Charities Newsroom."

16. "Better Ingredients. Better Pizza. Papa John's" (November 5, 2009), You-Tube video, posted by "PJ Tampa Bay," available from: https://www.youtube.com/watch?v=GHV8rZX4k8A&feature=related.

17. Dave Hendrick, "The Economist Names UVA Darden No. 1 Education Experience in US for Ninth Consecutive Year," Darden School of Business, November 2, 2019, available from: https://news.darden.virginia.edu/2019/11/02/no-1-education-experience-in-us/.

18. Patrick Barwise and Seán Meehan, "Bullseye: Target's Cheap Chic Strategy," Harvard Business School Working Knowledge, August 16, 2004, available from: http://hbswk.hbs.edu/archive/4319.html.

19. Lindsey Unterberger, " 'Darling, I'm Having the Most Extraordinary Experience . . . I'm Head over Heels in Dove!' As the Beauty Bar Turns 60, We Look Back on the Vintage Ads That Helped Make It a Household Name," DailyMail.com, January 10, 2007, available from: https://www.dailymail.co.uk/femail/article-4103774/Darling-m-having-extra-ordinary-experience-m-head-heels-Dove-beauty-bar-turns-60-look-vintage-ads-helped-make-household-name.html.

20. DesignCrowd, "Old and Classic Ads—100 Year Evolution of Print Ads," December 14, 2015, available from: https://blog.designcrowd.com/article/269/the-100-year-evolution-of-print-ads.

21. Kevin Roberts, *Lovemarks* (New York: Powerhouse Books, 2005), 33.

22. DesignCrowd, "Old and Classic Ads."

23. DesignCrowd, "Old and Classic Ads."

24. Cone, "Americans Willing to Buy or Boycott Companies Based on Corporate Values, According to New Research by Cone Communications," May 15, 2017, available from: http://www.conecomm.com/news-blog/2017/5/15/americans-willing-to-buy-or-boycott-companies-based-on-corporate-values-according-to-new-research-by-cone-communications.

25. Ward Alsop, "The Real Beauty of Brand Commodity," Endor by Design, April 2014, available from: https://endormedia.co.za/the-real-beauty-of-brand-continuity-dove-does-it-right/.

26. Kamau High, "Advocacy Group Blasts Unilever's 'Hypocrisy,'" *Adweek*, October 11, 2007, available from: https://www.adweek.com/brand-marketing/advocacy-group-blasts-unilevers-hypocrisy-90630/.

27. Tim Nudd, "Audi Defends Its Super Bowl Ad about Equal Pay after It Quickly Becomes a Flashpoint," *Adweek*, February 3, 2017, available from: https://www.adweek.com/brand-marketing/audi-defends-its-super-bowl-ad-about-equal-pay-after-it-quickly-becomes-a-flashpoint/.

28. Cone, "Americans Willing to Buy or Boycott Companies."

29. iSpot, "Olay Whips TV Commercial, 'The #1 Skincare Product in 2018?,'" available from: https://www.ispot.tv/ad/d6BX/olay-whips-the-1-skincare-product-in-2018.

4. Strategy Map Types

This chapter was coauthored with Kirstin DiCecca.

1. Robert S. Kaplan and David P. Norton, "Having Trouble with your Strategy? Then Map It," *Harvard Business Review*, September 2000, available from: https://hbr.org/2000/09/having-trouble-with-your-strategy-then-map-it.

2. Kenichi Ohmae, *The Mind of the Strategist* (New York: McGraw-Hill, 1982).

3. BCG, "What Is the Growth Share Matrix?" 2019, available from: https://www.bcg.com/about/our-history/growth-share-matrix.aspx.

4. BCG, "What Is the Growth Share Matrix?"

5. Jared D. Harris and Michael J. Lennox, *The Strategist's Toolkit* (Charlottesville, VA: Darden Business Publishing, 2013).

6. Derrick Daye, "Brand Positioning and Perceptual Maps," *Branding Strategy Insider*, September 1, 2009, available from: https://www.brandingstrategyinsider.com/2009/09/brand-positioning-and-perceptual-maps.html#.WibaZ0qnFPZ.

7. Balanced Scorecard Institute, "Balanced Scorecard Basics," available from: http://www.balancedscorecard.org/BSC-Basics/About-the-Balanced-Scorecard.

8. *McKinsey Quarterly*, "Enduring Ideas: The Strategic Control Map," McKinsey, July 1, 2010, available from: https://www.mckinsey.com/business-functions/strategy-and-corporate-finance/our-insights/enduring-ideas-the-strategic-control-map.

9. *McKinsey Quarterly*, "The New Metrics of Corporate Performance: Profit per Employee," McKinsey, February 1, 2007, available from: https://www.mckinsey.com/business-functions/strategy-and-corporate-finance/our-insights/the-new-metrics-of-corporate-performance-profit-per-employee.

10. Harris and Lennox, *The Strategist's Toolkit*.

5. The Strategic Marketing Plan

1. "The Purpose of Strategy is to Win: An Interview with A. G. Lafley," n.d., Korn Ferry.com https://www.kornferry.com/insights/articles/575-the-purpose-of-strategy-is-to-win-an-interview-with-a-g-lafley.

2. Kenneth Andrews, *The Concept of Corporate Strategy* (Homewood, IL: Richard D. Irwin, 1971), 18.

3. Michael E. Porter, "What Is Strategy?" *Harvard Business Review* (November–December 1996): 60–79.

4. CHRO = chief human resources officer; CIO = chief information officer; CFO = chief finance officer.

5. CTO = chief technology officer; CAO = chief administrative officer.

6. For a detailed, step-by-step sequence of activities in the strategic planning process, see L. J. Bourgeois (2013), "Developing a Strategy," in *UVA-S-0232* (Charlottesville, VA: Darden Business Publishing).

7. Walter Hickey and Grace Wyler, "Here's Everything We Know Now about Mitt Romney's Economic Plan," *Business Insider*, October 4, 2012, available at: http://www.businessinsider.com/romney-debate-economic-plan-2012-10.

6. The Creative Brief

1. Howard Ibach, *How to Write an Inspired Creative Brief* (iUniverse, 2009), 2.

2. Mark Duffy, "Creative Briefs: The Worst Pieces of Communication in History," *Digiday*, June 3, 2016, available from: https://digiday.com/marketing/marketing-briefs-worst-pieces-communication-history/.

3. Some firms have an internal agency, while others use an external agency. For the purposes of this discussion, the examples here focus on the client/external agency model. However, the relationship between a client and an internal agency would be largely the same.

4. This example is fictional, created for illustrative purposes only.

5. John Deighton, "Dove: Evolution of a Brand," Harvard Business School case 9-508-047, 2008. Available at: https://store.hbr.org/product/dove-evolution-of-a-brand/508047.

6. "About Dove," available from: http://www.dove.us/Social-Mission/campaign-for-real-beauty.aspx; David Aaker, "Dove: The Most Impressive Brand Builder," *Prophet*, May 1, 2013, available from: https://www.prophet.com/blog/aakeronbrands/138-dove.

7. This example was created by the author by reviewing a number of sources and reverse engineering the creative brief from the advertising. Also see Richard Rosenbaum-Elliott, Larry Percy, and Simon Pervan (2007), *Strategic Brand Management*, 4th ed. (Oxford: Oxford University Press), 72; "Case Study: MasterCard 'Priceless' New York," Lamar.com, available from: http://www.lamar.com/GetInspired/CaseStudies/Mastercard.

8. "MasterCard Baseball Commercial" (2007) YouTube video, 0:32, posted by "itgirl2001," available from: https://www.youtube.com/watch?v=71KAO_bmc2o&feature=youtu.be.

9. Ibach, *How to Write an Inspired Creative Brief*.

7. The Marketing Technology Blueprint

This chapter was coauthored with Scott Vaughan.

1. Bruce Upbin, "The Web Is Much Bigger (and Smaller) Than You Think," *Forbes*, April 24, 2012, available from: https://www.forbes.com/sites/ciocentral/2012/04/24/the-web-is-much-bigger-and-smaller-than-you-think/#4ef6ca4f7619.

2. Ashu Garg, "MarTech and the Decade of the CMO," Foundation Capital, available from: https://foundationcapital.com/wp-content/uploads/2019/02/DotCMO_whitepaper.pdf.

3. This chapter was written in collaboration with Scott Vaughan, chief growth officer at Integrate, Inc.

4. Scott Brinker, "Marketing Technology Landscape Supergraphic: MarTech 5000 (Actually 7,400)," Chiefmartec.com, April 4, 2019, available from: https://chiefmartec.com/2019/04/marketing-technology-landscape-supergraphic-2019/.

5. Garg, "MarTech and the Decade of the CMO."

6. The information in this section comes from Scott Vaughan and Cynthia Gumbert, "The MarTech BLUEPRINT Imperative," presentation, MarTech Conference, San Francisco, March 31, 2015, available at: http://www.slideshare.net/MarTechConf/the-martech-blueprint-imperative.

8. Key Opinion Leader and Influencer Mapping

1. Maher Jaber, "5 Reasons Why Social Media Influencers Are the Future of Digital Marketing," MarTechseries.com, June 7, 2018 available from: https://martechseries.com/mts-insights/guest-authors/5-reasons-why-social-media-influencers-are-the-future-of-digital-marketing/.

2. WARC, "Unilever's Rules for Influencer Marketing," December 3, 2018, available from: https://www.warc.com/newsandopinion/news/unilevers_rules_for_influencer_marketing/41407?utm_source=daily-email-free-link&utm_medium=email&utm_campaign=daily-email-americas-prospects-20181203.

3. Author interview with Steven Chang in November 2017. Kimberly A. Whitler, "If KOLs Aren't Part of Your Marketing Strategy, You Need to Read This," *Forbes.com*, January 13, 2018, https://www.forbes.com/sites/kimberlywhitler/2018/01/13/if-kols-arent-part-of-your-marketing-strategy-you-need-to-read-this/?sh=4e4c2f5651a6

4. These cases are based on interviews I conducted in November 2017 with executives from China. See Whitler, "If KOLs Aren't Part of Your Marketing Strategy."

5. WARC, "Unilever's Rules for Influencer Marketing," WARC, March 12, 2018, https://www.warc.com/newsandopinion/news/unilevers_rules_for_influencer_marketing/41407.

9. Brand Measurement Methods

This chapter was co-authored with Ellen Regan

1. Rita Clifton, *Brands and Branding*, 2nd ed. (New York: Bloomberg Press, 2009), 4.

2. Jack Trout, "Peter Drucker on Marketing," *Forbes*, June 30, 2006, available from: http://www.forbes.com/2006/06/30/jack-trout-on-marketing-cx_jt_0703drucker.html.

3. Peter Dixon "Consumer Discretionary," in *U.S. Equity Sector 2017 Outlook: The Fruits of Disruption*, Fidelity, 2016, available from: https://docplayer.net/38487647-U-s-equity-sector-2017-outlook-the-fruits-of-disruption.html.

4. Fournaise Group, "73 Percent of CEOs Think Marketers Lack Business Credibility: They Can't Prove They Generate Business Growth," June 15, 2011, available from: https://www.fournaisegroup.com/marketers-lack-credibility/.

5. Kusm L. Ailawadi, Donald R. Lehmann, and Scott A. Neslin (2003), "Revenue Premium as an Outcome Measure of Brand Equity," *Journal of Marketing* 67, no. 10 (2003): 1–17; Alice M. Tybout and Tim Calkins, *Kellogg on Branding* (Hoboken, NJ: Wiley, 2005).

6. Ailawadi et al., "Revenue Premium as an Outcome Measure of Brand Equity"; Tybout and Calkins, *Kellogg on Branding*.

7. Clifton, *Brands and Branding*.

8. Kantar Millward Brown, "Brand Valuation Methodology," 2015, available from: http://www.millwardbrown.com/brandz/rankings-and-reports/top-global-brands/2015/methodology.

9. Kantar Millward Brown, "Brand Valuation Methodology."

10. Kantar Millward Brown (2015), "BrandZ Top 100 Most Valuable Global Brands," available from: http://www.millwardbrown.com/BrandZ/2015/Global/2015_BrandZ_Top100_Report.pdf.

11. Interbrand, "Methodology," available from: http://interbrand.com/best-brands/best-global-brands/methodology/.

12. Interbrand, "Methodology."

13. Interbrand, "Methodology."

14. Rita Clifton, Brands and Branding, 2nd ed. (New York: Bloomberg Press, 2009).

15. Brand Finance, "Explanation of the Methodology," available from http://brandirectory.com/methodology.

16. Brand Finance, "Explanation of the Methodology."

17. Y&R, "About BAV Group," available from: http://www.yr.com/BAV.

18. "Measuring Your Net Promoter Score," Net Promoter System, available from: http://www.netpromotersystem.com/about/measuring-your-net-promoter-score.aspx.

19. "Measuring Your Net Promoter Score."

20. Kevin Lane Keller and Vanitha Swaminathan, Strategic Brand Management: Building, Measuring, and Managing Brand Equity, 5th ed. (Englewood Cliffs, NJ: Pearson Education, 2019).

21. Mindtools, "Keller's Brand Equity Model," available from: https://www.mindtools.com/pages/article/keller-brand-equity-model.htm.

22. Harris Poll, "2019 Harris Poll EquiTrend Study," available from: https://theharrispoll.com/equitrend/.

23. Harris Poll, "2019 Harris Poll EquiTrend Study."

24. Harris Poll, "2019 Harris Poll EquiTrend Study."

25. Harris Poll, "The 100 Most Visible Companies," 2019, available from: http://www.theharrispoll.com/reputation-quotient/.

26. https://theharrispoll.com/axios-harrispoll-100/

27. William R. Dillon, Dave Singleton, and Piotr Dworak, "Building Brand Attachment and Customer Value with Social Media," presented at the Customer Engagement Conference at Southern Methodist Univeristy (SMU), Cox School of Business, Dallas.

28. Dillon et al., "Building Brand Attachment and Customer Value with Social Media."

10. Activating Brand Tools through Practice and Implementation

1. Kimberly A. Whitler, "A CEO's Dream Team (CMO and CIO): The Regal Entertainment Group Story," Forbes.com, November 8, 2013, available from: https://www.forbes.com/sites/kimberlywhitler/2013/11/08/a-ceos-dream-team-cmo-and-cio-the-regal-entertainment-group-story/#5e4996fd1d4b.

2. Talkwalker, "7 Top Influencer Campaigns," November 13, 2018, available from: https://www.talkwalker.com/blog/top-7-influencer-campaigns-2018.

Index

239

Clifton, Rita, 41, 179
CMOs. *See* chief marketing officers
CoatChex. *See* Hoosier Coat Check
Coca-Cola, 13, 41, 186; BES exercise
    for, 209–214, *210, 211, 212*; brand
    architecture for, 213–214
Comcast, 49
commercials. *See* advertisements
communications, 30, 45, 212–213;
    brand-consumer, 123, 125, 167; in
    creative briefs, 129–130, 134–137;
    visual, 73–74, 94–95, 155, 158, 160,
    215, 221. *see also* advertisements
Di Como, Luis, 166, 172
companies, 70; acquisition targets
    for, 90–92, 161–164; decision-
    making by, 45–47, 75, 92–93, *93*;
    market capitalization of, 90–92;
    performance measures for, 89–90,
    91; reputations of, 43, 48–49. *See
    also* brands
competitive differentiation, 36–37,
    62–63139, 183
competitor brands, 62–63, 183, 214,
    225; in payoff matrices, 92–93, *93*;
    positioning concepts of, 14, 29
comp mentality, 94
concept development. *See* positioning
    concepts
concept development team, 23, 26,
    38; consumer-framed problems for,
    27–31; solution statements by, 27
concept-product fit, 30, 37
consulting firms, 62, 215. *See also*
    advertising agencies
consumer-brand relationships, 66–68,
    179–180, 193–194, *194*; influencer
    marketing and, 172–173
consumer-facing interfaces, 220–221
consumer-framed problems, 27, 31;
    rational benefits and, 55

consumer insights, 19, 21; for creative
    briefs, 129, 133, 138; data on,
    25–26, 28, 29, 126; in positioning
    concepts, 23–24, 25, 207; in
    problem statements, 32–33
consumer package goods (CPG)
    industry, 3, 4, 7; creative briefs
    in, 124; product development in,
    22
consumer perspectives, 90, *91*, 181
consumers, 12, 34, 154; behavior of,
    43, 126, *181*, 184, *185*, 193; brand
    knowledge of, *181*, 182, *185*, 196;
    demographics of, 52, 74, 80, *81*;
    emotional benefits for, 55–56, 58,
    59–60, 61, *65*, 75, 138, 139, 210;
    experiences, 44, 49, 82, 155, 193,
    209; perceptual maps and, 76–77,
    78, 87–88, *88, 89*; preferences of,
    80–82, *81*, 87–88, *88, 89*; surveys
    for, 26, 33, 43, *91*, 197; target, 25,
    52, 167, 182. *See also* problems;
    rational benefits
control maps, strategic, 90–92
controversial advertisements, 66–67
copy. *See* language
core positioning, 28–29, 139, 207; of
    J. C. Penney, 42
CPG. *See* consumer package goods
    industry
creative briefs, *140*–142, 225;
    assignment briefs for, 124–125,
    128; for Benadryl, *146*; BESs
    and, 130–131; as bridging tools,
    13, 121–122; client-agency
    relationship for, *124*, 124–125,
    133–137; consumer insights for,
    129, 133, 138; CPG industry, 124;
    development process for, 125–127,
    126, 131–132; elements of,
    128–131; language for, 130–131,